The Aphorisms of Franz Kafka

The Aphorisms of Franz Kafka

Edited, introduced, and
with commentaries by

Reiner Stach

Translated by

Shelley Frisch

PRINCETON UNIVERSITY PRESS
PRINCETON AND OXFORD

First published in Germany by Wallstein Verlag under the title *"Du bist die Aufgabe": Aphorismen*, copyright © Wallstein Verlag, Göttingen, 2019

English translation copyright © 2022 by Princeton University Press

Published by Princeton University Press
41 William Street, Princeton, New Jersey 08540
99 Banbury Road, Oxford OX2 6JX

press.princeton.edu

ISBN 978-0-691-20592-2
ISBN (e-book) 978-0-691-23639-1

British Library Cataloging-in-Publication Data is available

Editorial: Anne Savarese and James Collier
Production Editorial: Jill Harris
Jacket and Text Design: Chris Ferrante
Production: Erin Suydam
Publicity: Alyssa Sanford and Carmen Jimenez
Copyeditor: Molan Goldstein

Figure credits: (*page xii*) Photo: Archive of Jan Jindra; (*page 10*) The Bodleian Libraries, University of Oxford, MS. Kafka 43, No. 5; (*page 11*) The Bodleian Libraries, University of Oxford, MS. Kafka 25, fol. 5v; (*page 70*) The Bodleian Libraries, University of Oxford, MS. Kafka 43, No. 36; (*page 71*) The Bodleian Libraries, University of Oxford, MS. Kafka 25, fol. 21v; (*page 164*) The Bodleian Libraries, University of Oxford, MS. Kafka 43, No. 83; (*page 165*) The Bodleian Libraries, University of Oxford, MS. Kafka 25, fol. 34v; (*page 192*) The Bodleian Libraries, University of Oxford, MS. Kafka 43, No. 96; (*page 193*) The Bodleian Libraries, University of Oxford, MS. Kafka 26, fol. 3v.

Jacket image: Weerachai Khamfu / Shutterstock

This book has been composed in Garamond Premier Pro

Printed on acid-free paper. ∞

Printed in the United States of America

10 9 8 7 6 5 4 3 2 1

Contents

Translator's Note

After translating Reiner Stach's magnificent three-volume Kafka biography—published by Princeton University Press—I have now had the pleasure of returning to Franz Kafka, to Reiner Stach, and to the Press to work on this new annotated edition of Kafka's aphorisms. Translating this slim but seminal volume has deepened my understanding of all of Kafka's writings, even after the extremely deep dive I did for the biography.

The Aphorisms of Franz Kafka is not the first translation into English of Kafka's "Zürau aphorisms," but this new edition differs from all older ones in two notable respects. First and foremost, Reiner Stach's meticulous and astute interpretive guidance, which follows the translation of each aphorism, situates the individual aphorisms within the larger context of Kafka's writings and in doing so sheds light on both the elusive aphorisms themselves and the entirety of Kafka's oeuvre. My challenge here was to pick up on the nexus of interconnections that Reiner Stach laid out in his commentaries and take a fresh approach to the translations of the aphorisms with these interconnections in mind. The German word *Weg*, for example, traces a path throughout the aphorisms and is a significant connecting thread, which unspools when the word—which can mean *way, route, road*, et cetera—is rendered in a variety of ways, as it has been in previous translations. My translation, which uses *path* throughout, underscores the linkages between the aphorisms. As Andrew Hui points out in *A Theory of the Aphorism: From Confucius to Twitter*, "aphoristic writing can become a recursive exercise of saying the same thing in many different ways. Its concision invites repetitions and modulations. But this repetition is never sterile . . . it functions as an intensification of the problems at hand, affording discovery and experimentation."[1]

We learn from Stach's commentary that *Einpfählen*, in Aphorism 2, is a word that Kafka presumably knew from horticulture, and "refers to the use of posts to prop up and stabilize young fruit trees with (usually three) posts or to the use of fence posts to enclose a pasture. Kafka had ample opportunity to observe this work in Zürau." Hence, it is more specific in its origins and imagery than the *pinning down* one might find in other renderings of this aphorism. Stach's details about the dating and updating

---

1 Andrew Hui, *A Theory of the Aphorism: From Confucius to Twitter* (Princeton University Press, 2020), 20. Hui also notes the experience readers have come to associate with reading aphoristic writings, "The irony is that the aphorism—this shortest of forms to read—actually takes the longest time to understand" (p. 6).

of the aphorisms clue us in to the evolution of Kafka's thought and what he was reacting to at the time of their composition. An aphorism such as number 93 ("Psychology, for the last time!")—which scarcely fits the category of "aphorism" at all—cries out for context, and here, again, the annotations connect this potentially baffling outburst to Kafka's readings at the time, his correspondence, and his overall outlook on psychology. And by learning the details of Kafka's revisions, we gain deeper insight into Kafka's conceptual grapplings, such his choice of "invalid" (*nichtig*) after trying out and rejecting "incorrect," then "false," for Aphorism 6.

A second feature of this new edition is its inclusion of Kafka's original German for each of the aphorisms, thus furnishing readers who know German with still more interpretive tools. Kafka's aphorisms can be so cryptic that the discerning reader stands to benefit from every possible route of entry to them. In this bilingual edition, word usages and repetitions can be tracked in both languages. The inclusion of the original German wording serves to highlight where Kafka was tugging at the borders of "proper" German (*Alle menschlichen Fehler sind Ungeduld*: "All human errors are impatience") and has allowed my translations of the aphorisms to adhere more closely to Kafka's wording without seeming off—or *more* off, at any rate—than they appeared in German.

We have come a long way from Max Brod's original packaging of the aphorisms under the title *Reflections on Sin, Suffering, Hope, and the True Way*, which nudged Kafka's words in the theological direction Brod hoped to take them. We can now grasp anew the meaning of these enigmatic aphorisms—which many readers of Kafka consider the core, and jewel, of his oeuvre as a whole—while enhancing our understanding of Kafka's letters, diaries, short prose, and novels. I hope and trust that readers of this richly annotated volume will enjoy poring over it as much as I have enjoyed translating Franz Kafka's aphorisms and Reiner Stach's eye-opening commentaries.

Shelley Frisch
Princeton, New Jersey
June 2021

Foreword

Kafka's aphorisms are among the most original intellectual creations of the twentieth century, yet no aim is more alien to them than to drive home a point, produce an unprecedented effect, or astound an imagined readership. Exaggeration for the sake of effect—which we might think inherent in the literary genre of the aphorism—is barely in evidence here; even where well-versed readers expect it, where they savor their anticipation of it, Kafka almost always sacrifices aesthetic effect in favor of a maximal linguistic and visual compactness, right to the edge of comprehensibility and sometimes even a step beyond, which makes these texts forbidding, inscrutable. They show nothing, demonstrate nothing, move along their trajectory as they follow the path of an idea. And even the occasional *you* is not directed at us; it is the monological *you* that emerges from a state of deep concentration.

Some readers of Kafka have been mightily disappointed. Having learned to navigate, and derive aesthetic pleasure from, the world of "The Metamorphosis" and *The Trial*, which is marked in equal measure by nightmarish logic and humor, they can find their expectations dashed here; apart from a few incomparably memorable images and paradoxes, they will have trouble recognizing *their* author. The same applies to readers who gauge Kafka by the repository of German aphorisms by Lichtenberg, Friedrich Schlegel, Novalis, Nietzsche, Karl Kraus, and Adorno. The aphorist Elias Canetti, drawing on his own reading experience, pinpointed the expectations of these readers when he noted: "The great aphorists read as though they had all known one another well." This was certainly not true of Kafka. He did not belong to any literary circle or club, let alone to the group of "great minds" whose conversations he listened to attentively without joining in.

This unique position brings us straight to an awkward definitional dilemma. In reading the collection of Kafka's short texts, which is generally published as *Aphorisms* or *Zürau Aphorisms*, we have trouble assigning the term "aphorism" to them, no matter how modern and open-minded an approach we adopt. It is hard to picture a self-respecting literary scholar agreeing to call an exclamation like the one in Aphorism 93 ("Psychology, for the last time!") an aphorism, yet Kafka considered it significant enough to single out for inclusion here from the chaotic set of his notes.

Leopards that break into a temple, a great billiards player who damages the table: this is narration, pure and simple, and it is left to the reader to puzzle over whether something is actually being conveyed (Aphorisms

20, 107). The crows in heaven (32): isn't that more of a parable? And although the cage in search of a bird (16) is Kafka's best-known and most often quoted "aphorism," it is most assuredly not an aphorism-without-quotation-marks, nor is it a parable or narrative, but more of a surreal concept, a purely visual reflection that sparks our thoughts solely by showing us something inverted and baffling. Kafka's aphorisms are a compilation of texts of the most varied form, tonality, and length, and whatever may be holding these texts together, it is certainly not their external structure. And so the question is: what justifies its publication as a collection?

Kafka's literary output was unusually prolific in 1917—a war year—thanks to a conspiratorial arrangement he had with his youngest sister, Ottla, who was also his confidante. Ottla had rented a tiny cottage at the Hradčany in Prague so she could meet with her lover and future husband, Josef David, at a safe distance from her unsuspecting parents. But David was serving in the army, and the cottage was now rarely used, so Ottla offered it to her brother as a place to write in the evenings. It was quiet up there on Alchemists' Alley, and very little coal (which was horrifically expensive) was needed to keep this single room at a tolerable temperature, sometimes until well after midnight.

Tucked away in this village, Kafka could not bring himself to complete one of the novels he had set aside, *The Man Who Disappeared* or *The Trial*, as his friend and impresario Max Brod and others had hoped. But he *was* able to generate a whole series of precise and compact short prose pieces in rapid succession, which he hastened to compile under the title *A Country Doctor* and send to his publisher, Kurt Wolff. In addition to the title story, this volume included "A Report to an Academy," "An Imperial Message," and "Up in the Gallery."

This heady phase was over by April, however, when his writing was stymied by a daunting combination of external factors. Kafka's professional demands at the Workers' Accident Insurance Institute increased in response to the war; Ottla moved to the northwest Bohemian village of Zürau (called Siřem today), over her parents' vigorous objections but with her brother's support, in order to manage a farming estate there; and Franz himself felt compelled to rent an inhospitable apartment in Palais Schönborn, which was too chilly and damp even for him, although he considered himself immune to colds.

An occurrence on the early morning of August 11, 1917, would change his life and writing more lastingly than any other: an intense pulmonary hemorrhage that caused him to cough up blood. The bleeding lasted only a few minutes, but this alarming episode was an almost certain sign that he had come down with tuberculosis. It was nothing out of the ordinary in one of the Central European cities where the standards of hygiene had deteriorated badly, and hardly unexpected for a civil servant who had to meet at his office with ailing and disabled men day after day, men who had arrived from the front with hopes of gaining state-financed rehabilitation. But Kafka wanted nothing to do with those kinds of external explanations. He was a staunch proponent of natural healing, and convinced that there was no such thing as coming down with a disease for no good reason. People who fell ill were those whose poor lifestyle choices had enfeebled them, and "lifestyle," as understood by the back-to-nature movement, was all-encompassing, comprising a person's work, food, clothing, movement, sexuality, and psychological disposition.

Notions of this kind gave Kafka the opportunity to integrate the shock of his illness into his own self-perception, that is, to construe tuberculosis as a logical consequence of his life over the preceding years. Teasing out the correct interpretation now seemed more important to him than rushing headlong into some sort of conventional remedy, as his friends were urging. For years—since his first encounter with Felice Bauer—he had been draining himself in a battle between the calling of marriage and the calling of writing, his longing for intimacy with a woman and his equally deep longing for the rapture of production, and this battle was still being waged. He had proved incapable of making a firm decision and putting an end to the senseless manner in which he was wearing himself out with this state of paralysis—and now tuberculosis had stepped in to decide things for him. "Sometimes it seems to me," he wrote to Max Brod, "that my brain and lungs came to an agreement without my knowledge. 'Things can't go on this way,' said the brain, and after 5 years the lungs declared that they were ready to help."[1]

Kafka felt relieved—even physically—by this turn of events, and he was sufficiently self-aware to grasp the reasons for his paradoxical sensation, albeit unaware of the apt Freudian term to describe it, "primary morbid gain." Becoming a patient meant being granted a special social status. Patients could not be forced to do anything at all, neither commit to marriage nor work overtime at the office, much less take the needs of his publishers, critics, and readers into account while writing, as Brod encouraged him to do every now and then. The patient bears the responsibility for himself, and for nothing or no one else. Kafka now wanted to embrace that responsibility at long last, come what may.

1 Letter to Max Brod, September 14, 1917 (*B3* 319f.)

Needless to say, the Workers' Accident Insurance Institute was not prepared to grant an early retirement to Kafka at the age of thirty-four, especially in view of the many vacancies caused by the war. But the institute did unhesitatingly grant him a sick leave that could be extended as needed, which gave Kafka the freedom to take some time to decide on the setting for his convalescence. A sanatorium was out of the question; an institution of this kind would make sense if the goal was to soothe his nerves, but he had no intention of discussing symptoms, medicines, and doctors with dozens of coughing and blood-spitting fellow sufferers. He argued to Brod that he could get healthy only where he felt comfortable, and that was in the country, where he could relish the outdoors, in peace and quiet, with people whose company he enjoyed. Spending time with Ottla in Zürau was the solution, as he saw it, and so did his sister; she unhesitatingly welcomed him into her austere household. On September 12, one month after the hemorrhage, Kafka arrived with a minimum of luggage, not suspecting that he would be spending the winter in Zürau and remaining there for a full eight months.

The second pending decision pertained to the crucial changes occurring within him, a decision that was far more difficult. Kafka felt that his tuberculosis had brought him to a fork in the road and presented him a choice with no clear sense of the consequences of the path he might select, but at the same time it offered him the rare chance to change course: "You have the opportunity, as far as this opportunity is at all possible, to make a new beginning. Don't throw it away. If you insist on digging deep, you won't be able to avoid the muck that will well up. But don't wallow in it.

ZÜRAU bei Saaz.

If the infection in your lungs is only a symbol, as you say, a symbol of the infection whose inflammation is called Felice and whose depth is called justification; if this is so then the medical advice (light air sun rest) is also a symbol. Take hold of this symbol."[2] Kafka entered these words on the first page of a new diary volume, three days after his arrival.

"[A]s far as this opportunity is at all possible": in typical fashion, he started with a caveat. Kafka knew that there are no absolute beginnings; rarely has an author captured, in such compelling images, the exhilarating yet appalling fact that no past is ever past. That is why the fresh start he longed for could not mean simply brushing aside his achievements over the previous year. Even in his *Country Doctor* stories, which he was still eager to see in book form as soon as possible (Wolff did not actually publish the volume until the spring of 1920, which so infuriated Kafka that he thought of switching publishers), it was clear that his pleasure in spinning yarns, in recounting, had been cast aside in favor of contemplation and strict succinctness. Even though he eventually acquiesced to the subtitle "Short Prose," Kafka was experimenting with the forms of parable and legend in this volume, and even the "Report to an Academy," which abounded in grotesque and sensory details, was actually more a self-critical report than a narrative. Then there was "Eleven Sons," which dispensed with plot altogether and consisted solely of monological assessments. This was no longer the "portrayal of my dreamlike inner life" that Kafka had insisted was his sole interest just three years earlier; this was an entirely different scheme. "I can still have passing satisfaction from works like *A Country Doctor*," he noted in Zürau, "provided I can still achieve something of the sort (highly improbable), but happiness only if I can raise the world into the pure, the true, and the immutable."[3]

If *A Country Doctor* had been published back in the fall of 1917, any knowledgeable reader would have noticed that this author had not only shifted gears but had embarked on a totally new path. His friends Max Brod, Felix Weltsch, and Oskar Baum were well aware of this change. They knew Kafka's latest texts from his occasional private readings and hoped that in Zürau he would reap a comparable harvest. Hadn't Kafka always complained that as long as he was hemmed in between the hours he spent at the office and his family obligations, he lacked the requisite freedom? "Having been dependent on others for the most part," he wrote a year *before* Zürau, "I have an infinite longing for self-reliance, independence, freedom

2 Diary, September 15, 1917 (*T* 831).
3 Diary, August 6, 1914, September 25, 1917 (*T* 546, 838).

in all directions." No sooner had he arrived in the village than he wrote a letter praising "freedom, freedom above all."[4]

So what did Kafka do with this newfound freedom? He planted vegetables, dug potatoes out of the ground, pitched in here and there when the hops were harvested, and assisted in mating the goats. Between these activities he passed many hours lying in a lounge chair and reading in the blazing sun, then wrapped himself in blankets. In the evenings he composed witty, almost boisterous letters depicting the ascetic village life and a few tentative social contacts he had made, and spent quite a few pages describing the legions of mice that plagued him at night in his room. As entertaining as this writing was, these were not the stories that people back in Prague were hoping for from him. Even with a potentially deadly disease in his body, Kafka spoke and lived as though he had an infinite amount of time at his disposal.

But in reality, Kafka led a double, and even a triple, life in Zürau, which no one besides him could get a full picture of while he was there but which can now be reconstructed from the written records. In the view of the villagers, Kafka was the "Herr Doktor" from Prague, unfailingly friendly and cooperative, though not very talkative and therefore hard to read, and not in the best of health, as they could tell from his shortness of breath rather than from his appearance. In the view of his friends in Prague, he was now the author of some comic mouse letters, who on occasion also wrote about the books he was reading and provided lengthy yet cryptic remarks about his tuberculosis. These letters alarmed their recipients, as the patient seemed to be spending far more time and energy on *interpreting* his illness than on *recovering* from it.

And then there was a third, hidden dimension of his life in Zürau, the significance of which not even his sister may have been aware, involving two nondescript octavo notebooks, about 16.5 × 10 centimeters, with penciled scribblings that extended into the margins, generally in the slapdash penmanship that revealed he was writing in a lounge chair, his texts riddled with horizontal lines, shorthand symbols, and countless revisions. Occasionally there was a date, a comment about a long walk, or some brief stabs at narratives, but his entries most often consisted of reflective prose that abounded in startling images and metaphysical speculations.

This, then, was the "beginning" that Kafka had prescribed for himself—the continuation of a movement toward abstraction, as was already evident

---

4 Letter to Felice Bauer, October 19, 1916 (*B3* 261). Letter to Max Brod, September 14, 1917 (*B3* 319).

in the stories in *A Country Doctor* (we even find conceptual and visual fore-shadowings of the aphorisms in that volume), but now he did so with the utmost determination, crossing the boundaries of literature and heading up to the pinnacles that defined Western metaphysics as he engaged in speculations about "evil," "truth," "belief," and the "world of the spirit." Kafka's notes invoked an awe-inspiring term for these topics, calling them "the ultimate things," and he had no qualms about claiming a little pathos for himself in this sphere as well. "What I have to do, I can do only alone," he assured Brod during a visit in Prague in late December, "gain clarity about the ultimate things."[5] That sounded as though Kafka was intent on justifying his painful, yet merciless parting from Felice Bauer—which had just occurred—and his undertaking sounded like a new endeavor that would brook no compromises. He was actually talking about a project that had been underway for months, the initial product of which was concealed in two ordinary little notebooks.

In comparison with Kafka's other writings, his aphorisms have been over-looked by researchers and even more by his general readership. The aphorisms, like everything Kafka wrote, require interpretation, but in contrast to his fictional prose, for example *The Trial*, they do not reward the reader with the sensory and aesthetic pleasure of a story. Readers of the aphorisms wind up in unfamiliar, sometimes inhospitable territory, which can then turn terribly beautiful. "I have never been in this place before: breathing works differently, and a star shines next to the sun, more dazzlingly still." Kafka might as well have placed this aphorism—designated number 17— at the beginning, to serve as the motto for the entire collection. And there can be no doubt that quite a few of his devotees gave up trying to read these aphorisms, sighing, "This is too far removed from the world."

Kafka created this collection on his own, which is astonishing in view of the carelessness with which he usually treated his manuscripts (though not his galley proofs). Possibly while he was still in Zürau, that is, in the spring of 1918, he undertook a thorough assessment of his notes in the two octavo notebooks. He started by dividing a set of thin sheets of writing paper into four parts, thus yielding a stack of sheets measuring 14.5 × 11.5 centimeters. Then he went through the octavo notebooks page by page and copied individual notes in ink, in chronological sequence, one per sheet,

5 Max Brod, Diary, December 26, 1917 (National Library of Israel, Jerusalem). Otto Weininger's literary remains, with which Kafka was definitely acquainted, were published in 1904 as *Über die letzten Dinge* [On the ultimate things].

which he had numbered in advance, and in quite a few cases he revised the texts even in the course of copying them. A total of 105 of these sheets are extant. The first two are housed with Max Brod's literary estate at the National Library of Israel in Jerusalem; the others, including the octavo notebooks, are kept in the Bodleian Library in Oxford. The last sheet bears the number 109, and we don't know to what extent that number resulted from errors in the numbering process or from the disappearance of individual sheets. (For more on the irregularities of the numbering, see the individual commentaries.)

As usual, Kafka appears not to have shown these texts to anyone (see the commentary on Aphorism 69), but he did not lay them aside. He crossed out a total of twenty-three aphorisms on the sheets—it is unclear when this occurred—without removing them from the bundle. In fall 1920 at the earliest, that is, two and a half years after writing the texts on the sheets, Kafka added supplementary texts, which he copied from a different, newer notebook. For these additional texts—eight in all—he did not make separate sheets but instead used the ones that were already there.

The genesis of this project is complex and highly unusual for Kafka, who hardly ever copied his own texts by hand, and raises the question of why he did so. It is of course conceivable that he simply sought to preserve the fruits of his labor in Zürau. Even he must have had difficulty reading the notes fluently as he went over the octavo notebooks, and he surely found it harder still to identify and organize the scattered musings on a specific topic. The sheets could be regarded as a linguistic and notional extract, prepared in a form that made it feasible to track them down again, although the numbering of the sheets wouldn't have been strictly necessary, aside from serving as a tool to rearrange the aphorisms by topics. The numbers also are one indication—indeed, the *only* indication—that Kafka was, at least intermittently, considering the idea of publishing the sheets, while his elimination of this ordering principle by doubling up on the use of the sheets shows that by late 1920 he had given up his plan for publication but wanted to preserve particularly significant yields of his contemplations about "the ultimate things."

The reception of the aphorisms began in 1931, with the publication of the anthology *The Great Wall of China*, edited by Max Brod. In order to reinforce Brod's own slant on this work—he regarded Kafka as a reviver of Jewish religiosity—Brod chose the suggestive, optimistic title *Reflections on Sin, Suffering, Hope, and the True Path*. That title raised misgivings among readers and academic critics from the outset, but they lacked any knowledge of the context in which the aphorisms had been written. The (almost) complete Zürau octavo notebooks, now called *Octavo Notebooks*

G and *H*, were not published until 1953.[6] Critical editions that appeared in print in 1992/93 and 2011 revealed the revision processes[7] and shed light, at long last, on the mysterious sheets.

It turned out that the chaotic Zürau notes are virtually indispensable to an understanding of the central motifs and concepts of the aphorisms, but the set of pages as a whole cannot be reconfigured to signify a revival of a tradition, much less as a doctrine that could establish a tradition or provide signposts. Kafka was sketching a kind of ideological blueprint with a theological underpinning, yet his concepts remain hazy, because the evolution of a given idea often adheres to a purely visual logic. The boundaries between "the good," "the true," "the divine," and "the indestructible" are fluid; at times these are synonyms, at others they are not, depending on the context. This conceptual fluidity undermines any efforts to reconcile these terms with their meanings in other contexts in a straightforward manner. "Good" in Kafka is not the same as in Plato or in Christianity, despite the obvious lines of influence. We know that Kafka read Kierkegaard's writings while in Zürau, yet the contours of his outlook on life were clearly discernible in the octavo notebooks, quite a while before February 1918, when his intensive reading of Kierkegaard began, so we cannot know whether he was seeking instruction or confirmation in Kierkegaard, in which works he was looking for what, and how aware he was of what he was hoping to find. While it may be exciting to come across a comment in Kierkegaard suggesting that "the ethical is just as boring in life as it is in learning,"[8] which instantly brings to mind Kafka's baffling Aphorism 30 ("In a certain sense the Good offers no comfort"), the value of these sorts of isolated findings in gaining an understanding of Kafka's sometimes inscrutable statements is limited, since the backgrounds of the two authors were so very different. Consequently, the commentaries in this edition always give priority to the numerous connections *between* Kafka's notations.

Similarly, Kafka's "truth" is clearly not the kind found in Judaism or one of its mystical movements. Covert relationships to the Kabbalah or to Hasidism have been the subject of detailed studies of Kafka's writings for

6 In Franz Kafka, *Hochzeitsvorbereitungen auf dem Lande und andere Prosa aus dem Nachlass*. Vol. 9 of Franz Kafka, *Gesammelte Werke*, ed. Max Brod (Frankfurt am Main: S. Fischer, 1953), 55–161.

7 See *NSF1, NSF2, 8°Ox7, 8°Ox8*. Stroemfeld Verlag produced a cardboard box containing facsimiles of the sheets Kafka used to write these aphorisms in conjunction with its publication of the historical-critical edition of his works.

8 Søren Kierkegaard, *Either/Or: A Fragment of Life*, trans. Alastair Hannay (New York: Penguin, 1992), 263.

a good many years,[9] but here, too, we need to be careful not to take the correspondences too literally, without regard to their literary reshaping. Kafka adopted or scrutinized particular conceptual frameworks that he found substantive, but he employed the underlying theological vocabulary in a distanced, metaphorical manner—even when he used the word "God." In the *Kafka-Handbuch* (2010), co-editor Manfred Engel gets to the heart of the matter when he concludes, "Kafka's position has little to do with established religious concepts. He appears to be focused on an extremely reduced religion, stripped bare of dogmatic content, religion as *re-ligio*, as a *re-binding* to an unspecified transempirical principle."[10]

This proviso applies even when Kafka refers directly to established mythologems, to their iconography and interpretive tradition. One striking example is the double motif of "Paradise/Fall of man," which appears in eight of the aphorisms and numerous other notes he wrote in Zürau. As we learn from Kafka's diary, about a year before he fell ill, Kafka had immersed himself in the Old Testament, especially in the book of Genesis, and his remarkable summary read: "Only the Old Testament sees—say nothing yet about it."[11] The biblical account of the expulsion from Paradise is accordingly not just one of the clearly identifiable sources of the aphorisms but also a significant influence on the content of Kafka's writing.

But this influence does not furnish proof that Kafka was following an established tradition or even feeling indebted to it. It was quite the opposite: he would take up a motif that he deemed significant and attempt to make it conform to his own conceptual framework; filmmakers would call this a recut version. For example, the Tree of Life, which in the Bible is merely a secondary motif, becomes a key point in Kafka's retelling, in the most astonishing manner. If we combine the logic of Aphorisms 82 and 83, which mention the Tree of Life, we find that God *forced* man to continue a sin of omission (namely to commit the sin of *not* eating from the Tree of Life), which does not invert the plot but does turn the moral import of the narrative on its head.

---

9 The chapter "Reflections from a Damaged Life: The Zürau Aphorisms, 1917–1918" in Ritchie Robertson, *Kafka: Judaism, Politics, Literature* (New York: Oxford University Press, 1985), 185–217, is still quite informative on this subject. The most ambitious attempt at classifying Kafka's Zürau notes in the framework of intellectual history is Paul North's *The Yield: Kafka's Atheological Reformation* (Palo Alto: Stanford University Press, 2015).

10 Manfred Engel and Bernd Auerochs, eds., *Kafka-Handbuch: Leben—Werk—Wirkung* (Stuttgart: J. B. Metzler, 2010), 288.

11 Diary, July 6, 1916 (*T* 792).

In other notes too, Kafka treats the text that has been passed down through the ages like an interesting script that could use some improvement. He remarks, for example, that the Creator makes unpersuasive threats: "According to God, the immediate consequence of eating of the Tree of Knowledge was to be death; according to the serpent (or at least it could be understood this way), becoming like God. Both were wrong in similar ways," and the fact that both were also "right in similar ways" doesn't do much to improve matters.[12] This is a clear example of Kafka's characteristically freewheeling use of mythological elements, never arbitrary but certainly irreverent; see, for example, "Prometheus" and "The Silence of the Sirens," two texts that also form part of his writings in Zürau.

"Only the Old Testament sees"—this odd wording accordingly does not mean that the biblical text *expresses* truth but rather that it *refers* to something true in a visually striking manner, similar to the effect of a work of pictorial art. In Kafka's view, something took place in the history of mankind for which the "expulsion from Paradise" is an apt, intellectually productive, and vivid ascription, a kind of ontological fall from a perfect state to a far less perfect one.

But this is where the parallel to Judeo-Christian mythology ended, and Kafka carried his idea further. According to the myth, the Fall took place *once*, far back in the past. That is illogical, Kafka said. Paradise is part of a sphere of eternity that bears no relation to our concepts of time, and our notion that life in Paradise is over and done with merely reflects our limited point of view. Kafka launched into a speculative feat that does not get any easier to grasp by seeking parallels or influences in the history of ideas, but only by tracking the many visual and conceptual relations *between* his Zürau notes. Are we then able to extract a systemic idea from all this?

One of the central propositions that are advanced in the aphorisms, some of which are addressed explicitly while others remain implicit, harks back to Plato's theory of forms, in which Kafka had been exceptionally well versed since his high school years. It states that there is a world of the spirit and a world of the senses, a world of ideas and a world of phenomena. The world that is familiar to us is the world of the senses, and we typically believe that it is the only one, yet it is really only a kind of shadow, lacking any substance of its own, a dim reflection of the world of the spirit. For this reason, the aphorisms continually speak of two entirely different worlds while insisting that there is actually only one: that of the spirit (see Aphorisms 54 and 62). For this reason alone, it would be misleading to imagine

12 *NSF2* 73 / *8°Ox7*, 140–143.

the two worlds as adjacent spaces: this world over here, the world beyond over there.

How, then, are we to understand all this? For Kafka, the two worlds seem to have a complex relationship, comprising both inclusive and exclusive connections. He concluded, for instance, that the justification for our existence in the here and now is possible only in the world beyond, whereas everything we can do "here" seems to be predetermined from "beyond" (see Aphorism 99 and the commentary on Aphorism 94). And even though the world of the spirit is inaccessible to us, there is no actual border, and hence there are no border posts. It would be good to have a somewhat well-defined model for heuristic purposes.

Let us picture some faraway planet with creatures who possess both intelligence and consciousness, but whose bodies and consequently sensations and powers of imagination are limited to only two dimensions. Their physical and mental world is flat, two-dimensional. Everything here has only length and width, and the concept of "height" is meaningless to them.

If these creatures should start to believe that they are making out signs of a third dimension, something like a "higher world," and if they go on to wonder where this third dimension might be located, we could shout over to them: *Just look up, there it is, your higher world is close by!* But that would be of little use, because the concept of "up" has no experiential value in that world. No one there has ever looked up, because this direction doesn't appear to exist. This would not stop the flat-earthers, however, from visualizing the relationship of their level to the planetary system as a whole, at least theoretically (for instance by the use of analogies or mathematical theory), and even making accurate statements about it.

They would likely soon realize that although a sharp distinction had to be drawn between two-dimensional and three-dimensional space, the one is somehow still embedded in the other. There is "actually" only three-dimensional space, and the flat-earthers are in it as well, as they may be thinking without being able to picture it.

The parallels to Kafka's conceptual pairs, "sensory/spiritual" and "earthly/heavenly," are astounding, and so sweeping that it appears he was drawing on the didactic model of the different dimensions of space that was familiar from the theory of relativity. One example is Aphorism 64, which appears inexplicable, as it describes a situation that is utterly inconceivable: On the one hand, we have been expelled once and for all from the higher sphere of Paradise, while on the other, it is possible that we are still there, even unawares. Given the geometrical circumstances of the flat-earthers, this would not be a contradiction, and so they, too, could eventually, after philosophical reflection, reach the conclusion that they have already been living in that higher world and that it is simply up to their consciousness whether this has any consequences for their lives.

As indicated earlier, Kafka accounted for the odd simultaneity of seemingly irreconcilable elements in Aphorism 64 with the clash of two time structures. In the world of the spirit there is only timeless eternity, so it is not possible for any event to come to a definitive end, because then it would be in the past. The expulsion from Paradise should be pictured as an *ongoing event*, which once again brings Kafka into absolutely abstract territory. This seesawing between extreme abstraction and unfailingly compelling pictoriality is a key component of the aphorisms' substantial intellectual appeal.

But Kafka does not have a theory that could also be formulated in the categories of religious or philosophical discourse, of whatever nature. Anyone seeking to systematize Kafka's aphoristic legacy in this manner would soon realize that it was bound to fail, if for no other reason than the constant overlap between ontological, epistemological, and ethical concepts and arguments (see the commentary on Aphorisms 54 and 80). And inconsistencies would crop up on the spot—such as accusing those in Paradise of "impatience," even though they lived (or rather, *live*, Kafka would clarify; see Aphorism 3) in a world of eternity. These inconsistencies do not stem from Kafka's alleged inability to engage in abstract thinking; indeed, some of the aphorisms (such as 104) move about in the lofty heights of abstraction and require repeated rereadings to tease out their meaning. But even here, Kafka refrained from resorting to technical terminology. Instead, he found images for abstract concepts and consistently adhered to those images. They are not there to *illustrate* his arguments; they *are* his arguments.

The aphorisms are consequently literature—which raises the question of their place in Kafka's literary production. The assemblage of reflective texts in his late works is striking; the "Investigations of a Dog" (1922, title by Max Brod) is not a straight narrative but rather an analysis of experiences, and the same is true of the long story "The Burrow" (1923), which consists almost exclusively of reflections. The somewhat lesser popularity (compared with a work like *The Trial*) of *The Castle*, written in 1922, stems in part from the fact that its plot elements are continually interrupted by long passages of dialogue that circle in on themselves and ultimately come to a complete standstill. In *The Castle*, the speculative interpretation of the events, which in *The Trial* had been plucked out of the main narrative thrust and given a chapter of its own ("In the Cathedral" / "Before the Law"), becomes a *basso continuo* that dominates the atmosphere.

Kafka ultimately tried to tie up the two loose ends once again, to synthesize conceptual and visual thoughts with literary means and in vivid images. Readers of the aphorisms will recognize these images in *The Castle*, as structural rather than literal borrowings, as endeavors to rechannel the unimaginable to a sensory context and thereby render it ever so slightly more imaginable. The aphorisms envision a world of the senses and a world of the spirit, wherein the latter world is unattainable to us, yet everyone actually already lives within it. In *The Castle*, there is the village and there is the unapproachable castle, and yet: "This village is the property of the Castle, so anyone who lives or spends the night here is effectively living or spending the night at the Castle."[13] We are already well acquainted with this "effectively."

13 *S* 8.

Aphorisms and Commentary

Notes for the aphorisms and commentary can be found immediately following this section, on pages 223–228.

I

Der wahre Weg geht über ein Seil, das nicht in der Höhe gespannt ist, sondern knapp über dem Boden. Es scheint mehr bestimmt stolpern zu machen, als begangen zu werden.

The true path leads along a rope stretched, not high in the air, but barely above the ground. It seems designed more for stumbling than for walking along it.

Recorded on October 19, 1917. In the octavo notebook, this text opens with the words: "I digress. The true path . . ." Kafka later added the sentence that begins with "It seems designed more" to the octavo notebook, then copied it onto sheet 1. (See the foreword for information about Kafka's process of copying his texts.)[1]

Kafka appears to have found the motif of the rope in a Hasidic story he had recently read, in which two men sentenced to death are able to save their lives by walking along a rope stretched across a pond. When the first of them has made it to the other side, he says to the other: "The most important thing is not to forget for a second that you're walking on a rope and that your life is at stake." In this story, the rope serves as an explicit metaphor for the "path . . . to true worship," while Kafka relies on the logic of the image itself. As he sees it, the rope is literally lying on the path until such time as the decision is reached to walk on it.

For more on the path as metaphor, see Aphorisms 21, 26, 38, 39a, and 104.

Additional thematically related entries in the octavo notebooks are these: "The thornbush is the ancient barrier of the path. It must catch fire if you want to go farther." "The various forms of hopelessness at the various stations on the path." "He has too much spirit; he travels across the earth on his spirit as though he's on a magic chariot, even where there are no paths. And he cannot figure out on his own that there are no paths there. In this way his humble plea for others to follow him turns into tyranny, and his sincere belief that he is 'on the path' turns into haughtiness." "For me, the path to my fellow man is a very long one."

In a letter to his friend Robert Klopstock in the summer of 1922, Kafka continued to develop the metaphor of the true path: "but since we are only on a path that must first lead to a second one and this to a third and so on, and then the right one doesn't come for quite some time, and may never come at all . . ." In the same year, Kafka wrote his prose piece "A Commentary" (better known under the titles "Give Up" or "Give It Up"), in which a policeman is amused by the notion that he, of all people, would be asked about the right path. His reaction would be incomprehensible to us without knowledge of the deeper metaphorical meaning of the word.

---

1 *Translator's note:* The originals of these sheets of paper are 11 cm (4.33 inches) in length, and 14 cm (5.54 inches) wide, which makes them somewhat larger than what we normally regard as slips of paper (the standard definition of *Zettel*). Kafka cut full-size sheets into quarters for the purpose of these brief texts. Reiner Stach's foreword provides further details on Kafka's arrangement of the texts on paper, the numbering system, and other textual matters.

2

Alle menschlichen Fehler sind Ungeduld, ein vorzeitiges Abbrechen des Methodischen, ein scheinbares Einpfählen der scheinbaren Sache.

All human errors are impatience, a premature breaking off of a methodical approach, an apparent use of posts to prop up the apparent objective.

Recorded on October 19, 1917. In the octavo notebook, this text opens with "Psychology is impatience, all human errors are impatience . . ." The definitive message, which omits any mention of psychology, is thus the outcome of Kafka's decision to broaden the scope and thereby obscure the more limited sphere of reference.

These ideas were evidently prompted by a letter he had recently received from Felix Weltsch in which Weltsch tried to come to grips with Kafka's inconsistent behavior in psychological terms, particularly with regard to his illness. Kafka responded that Weltsch's remarks belonged "to that damned circuit of psychological theory, which you love, or rather which you don't love, but which obsesses you (and me apparently as well). The nature theories [?][1] are wrong, as are their psychological counterparts."

One day after writing this aphorism, Kafka returned to the more general theme of impatience and composed Aphorism 3.

Sheets 1 and 2 are the only ones that Max Brod published back in 1926 in *Die Literarische Welt* as facsimiles, and the only ones that are housed with Brod's literary estate at the National Library of Israel in Jerusalem instead of at the Bodleian Library in Oxford.

Kafka was presumably acquainted with the term *Einpfählen* from horticulture; it refers to the use of posts to prop up and stabilize young fruit trees with (usually three) posts or to the use of fence posts to enclose a pasture. Kafka had ample opportunity to observe this work in Zürau.

1 *Translator's note*: The question mark is in the original letter to Weltsch.

3

Es gibt zwei menschliche Hauptsünden, aus welchen sich alle andern ableiten: Ungeduld und Lässigkeit. Wegen der Ungeduld sind sie aus dem Paradiese vertrieben worden, wegen der Lässigkeit kehren sie nicht zurück. Vielleicht aber gibt es nur eine Hauptsünde: die Ungeduld. Wegen der Ungeduld sind sie vertrieben worden, wegen der Ungeduld kehren sie nicht zurück.

There are two cardinal human sins, from which all others derive: impatience and laxity. Impatience got them expelled from Paradise; indolence keeps them from returning. Perhaps, though, there is only one cardinal sin: impatience. Impatience got them expelled; impatience keeps them from returning.

Recorded on October 20, 1917. When Kafka copied the text onto sheet 3, he changed both instances of "banished" to "expelled." Afterward, however, he crossed out the entire text.

Aphorisms 64, 74, 82, and 84 also comment on the expulsion from Paradise. The topic had obviously been on Kafka's mind for quite some time; in the previous year he wrote to Felice Bauer about two idyllic spots he had discovered near Prague: "Both places silent as the Garden of Eden after the expulsion of man."

Additional thematically related entries in the octavo notebooks are these: "Adam's first house pet after the expulsion from Paradise was the serpent." "In one sense, the expulsion from Paradise was a stroke of luck, for if we had not been expelled, Paradise would have had to be destroyed." "According to God, the immediate consequence of eating of the Tree of Knowledge was to be death; according to the serpent (or at least it could be understood this way), becoming like God. Both were wrong in similar ways. Humans did not die but rather became mortal; they did not become like God, but they did receive an indispensable capacity to become so. Both were also correct in similar ways. Humans did not die, but paradisiac humans did; they did not become God, but did get divine knowledge." [all crossed out] "There were three possible ways of punishing man for the Fall: the mildest was the way it actually happened, the expulsion from Paradise / the second, the destruction of Paradise / the third—and this would have been the most terrible punishment—blocking off the Tree of Life and leaving all else unaltered." "If ... thou shalt die" means that knowledge is both at once: a step toward eternal life and an obstacle to it. If you wish to attain eternal life after having gained knowledge—and you will not be able to want otherwise, for knowledge is this will—you will have to destroy yourself, the obstacle, in order to build the steps; that is the destruction. The expulsion from Paradise was thus not an act but an event." [crossed out, with the exception of the last sentence]

4

Viele Schatten der Abgeschiedenen beschäftigen sich nur damit die Fluten des Totenflusses zu belecken, weil er von uns herkommt und noch den salzigen Geschmack unserer Meere hat. Vor Ekel sträubt sich dann der Fluss, nimmt eine rückläufige Strömung und schwemmt die Toten ins Leben zurück. Sie aber sind glücklich, singen Danklieder und streicheln den Empörten.

Many shades of the departed are occupied solely with lapping at the waters of the river of death because it comes from us and still bears the salty tang of our seas. Then the river writhes in revulsion, its current flowing backward, washing the dead back into life. But they are happy, sing hymns of thanksgiving, and caress the indignant river.

Recorded on October 20, 1917. The last sentence was added later in the octavo notebook.

Kafka had played with the motif of the river of death during the previous winter in the extensive fragments about Hunter Gracchus, who, though deceased, returns to the "earthly waters" as a result of "a wrong turn of the tiller."

Von einem gewissen Punkt an gibt s keine
Rückkehr mehr. Dieser Punkt ist zu erreichen.

was will ich tun? oder
Wozu will ich es tun? sind
keine Fragen dieser Gegenden. P|

manche Schatten der Ungeschehe-
lichkeiten. Und damit die
Fluten des ~~Totenstromes~~ Toten flusses
~~strom~~ zu belecken, weil
er ~~nicht~~ von mir herkommt

Und in salzigen Schwanz
vor Blut
~~thiere hat~~ Jahre
~~denn der~~ nimmt eine pickelartige
~~strummung und geschwemmt der Toten~~
~~weder Leben wieder~~

gibt es keine Rückkehr
mehr. Diese Furcht ist zu
erreichen

5

Von einem gewissen Punkt an gibt es keine Rückkehr mehr. Dieser Punkt ist zu erreichen.

From a certain point on, there is no turning back. This is the point that needs to be reached.

Recorded on October 20, 1917. In the octavo notebook, this sentence is singled out for emphasis by a vertical line in the margin.

How Kafka came upon this idea is unknown, but it is clearly applicable to several of his most pressing conflicts: the final separation from Felice Bauer, which he decided on in Zürau; disentangling himself from his father; and making the transition he yearned for from a middle-class existence to a life subject solely to the laws of writing.

It is notable how close this comes to Kafka's favorite metaphor of the "path." Stepping onto the rope in Aphorism 1 (which he had written the previous day) was also a critical juncture from which there was no turning back. And the protagonist of *The Castle* has also gone too far (in a literal as well as metaphorical sense) to return to the life he previously led.

Yet another parallel is evident in Kafka's use of the concept "threshold," such as in his 1922 diary entry: "Nothing evil; once you have crossed the threshold, all is good. Another world, and you needn't speak."

6

Der entscheidende Augenblick der menschlichen Entwicklung ist immer-
während. Darum sind die revolutionären geistigen Bewegungen, welche alles
Frühere für nichtig erklären, im Recht, denn es ist noch nichts geschehen.

The decisive moment of human development is everlasting. That is why
the revolutionary movements grounded in intellect, which deem invalid everything that has gone before, are correct, for as yet nothing has
happened.

Recorded on October 20, 1917. In the octavo notebook, the entry begins with the words: "The decisive moment in human development is when we drop our concept of time everlastingly. The history of mankind is the split second between two strides taken by a traveler."

Kafka crossed out this second sentence in the octavo notebook. At first he used the wording "when we drop our concept of time" when writing it on sheet 6, but then he crossed that out as well.

Moreover, it took him three tries in the octavo notebook to settle on the word "invalid" (*nichtig*). First he wrote "incorrect" (*unrichtig*), then "false" (*falsch*), then "invalid" (*nichtig*).

Soon afterward, Kafka varied the basic idea of this aphorism in a letter to Max Brod, but applied it to the life of the individual: "if there are not countless opportunities for liberation, but especially opportunities at every moment of our lives, then perhaps there are none at all."

The notion that we cannot trust our limited concept of time when pondering the destiny of mankind appears in Aphorism 64 as well.

7

Eines der wirksamsten Verführungsmittel des Bösen ist die Aufforderung zum Kampf. Er ist wie der Kampf mit Frauen, der im Bett endet.

One of the most effective means of seduction that Evil employs is the call to battle. It is like the battle with women, which ends in bed.

Recorded on October 20, 1917. In the octavo notebook, this passage was initially one sentence longer: "One of the most effective means of seduction employed by Evil is the call to battle. It is like the battle with women, which ends in bed. The true infidelities of a married man are—rightly understood—never merry."

After entering the revised and abridged version onto sheet 7, Kafka crossed out the entire text.

Evil is the most frequently recurring theme in Kafka's aphorisms; see 19, 28, 29, 39, 51, 54, 55, 85, 86, 95, 100, 105. The theme of female sexuality as an instrument of Evil is also found in Aphorism 105, where the "woman's gaze" explicitly represents "Good."

There are several additional thematically related entries in the octavo notebooks: "Evil is whatever distracts" and "Evil knows of Good, but Good does not know of Evil." "Only Evil has self-knowledge." "One resource Evil has at hand is the dialogue." "Evil is the starry sky of Good." "In Paradise as always: that which causes sin and that which recognizes it for what it is are one and the same. The clear conscience is Evil, which is so triumphant that it does not even consider that leap from left to right necessary any longer." "The comfortless horizon of Evil, thinking his god-like status is evident in the very fact of his knowledge of Good and Evil. The accursedness does not seem to worsen anything in his nature: he will measure out the length of the path with his belly."

*Eine stinkende Hündin, reichliche Kindergebärerin, stellenweise schon fau-
lend, die aber in meiner Kindheit mir alles war, die in Treue unaufhörlich
mir folgt, die ich zu schlagen mich nicht überwinden kann, vor der ich aber,
selbst ihren Atem scheuend, schrittweise nach rückwärts weiche und die mich
doch, wenn ich mich nicht anders entscheide, in den schon sichtbaren Mau-
erwinkel drängen wird, um dort auf mir und mit mir gänzlich zu verwesen,
bis zum Ende—ehrt es mich?—das Eiter- und Wurm-Fleisch ihrer Zunge
an meiner Hand.*

A stinking dog, mother of numerous pups, already rotting in spots, but
who was everything to me in my childhood, who follows me faithfully
all the time, whom I cannot bring myself to strike, yet I shrink back from
her, step by step, even avoiding her breath, and who will wind up driving
me into a corner, already in sight, if I don't decide otherwise, and rot away
altogether on me and with me until I end up with—does this dignify
me?—the pus-filled and worm-infested flesh of her tongue at my hand.

Recorded on October 21, 1917. This passage originally bore the title "A Life." Kafka retained the title as he wrote the text on sheet 8/9, but crossed it out there.

The text in the octavo notebook initially referred to a male dog (*Hund*). Only after completing it did Kafka replace all the masculine forms by feminine forms (*Hündin*, "her") and added the words "mother of numerous pups."

Kafka initially labeled this sheet number 8, and later added the number 9. He may have noticed that he had accidentally skipped over the number 9 while numbering the empty sheet. It is also conceivable, however, that there was a sheet that Kafka numbered 9 and later destroyed.

Max Brod found this passage so repugnant that he omitted it when first publishing the numbered aphorisms in 1931; he renumbered the aphorisms that followed to conceal the omission.

A. ist sehr aufgeblasen, er glaubt im Guten weit vorgeschritten zu sein, da er, offenbar als ein immer verlockenderer Gegenstand immer mehr Versuchungen aus ihm bisher ganz unbekannten Richtungen sich ausgesetzt fühlt. Die richtige Erklärung ist aber die, dass ein grosser Teufel in ihm Platz genommen hat und die Unzahl der kleineren herbeikommt, um dem Grossen zu dienen.

A. is quite full of himself, believing he is far advanced in goodness, since he feels that as an evident object of increasing attraction, he is exposed to more and more temptations from directions previously unknown to him. But the true explanation is that a great devil has taken up residence within him, and an immense number of lesser devils are coming by to serve the great one.

Recorded on October 22, 1917, just after the words "Morning in bed."

On the previous day, Kafka had written a prose piece that provides a narrative context for the motif of the devil living within a person. It opens with the words: "Sancho Panza, who, it should be said, never boasted of it, was able, over the course of years, in the evening and night hours, to divert his demon—whom he later dubbed Don Quixote—away from himself by amassing a great many chivalry romances and picaresque novels."

The notion of having one or several devils "of one's own" appears in many of Kafka's letters. In 1912 he explained in his diary why there are usually many of them. In the summer of 1913 he studied Gustav Roskoff's two-volume *History of the Devil* (1869).

Kafka found confirmation for the notion that good people are exposed to an especially broad range of temptations, but also have the means to outwit the devil, in a Hasidic story he heard in 1915: A chief rabbi orders his favorite student to convert to Christianity for the time being in order to "divert his demon." Thus, Evil is not only something "that diverts" (according to Kafka's definition); Evil itself can also be diverted.

"A." is not a real person here but rather a "someone," the abstract embodiment of a course of action or a human characteristic, as is evident from the following entry in the octavo notebook and in the associated revisions: "A.'s spiritual poverty and the torpor of this poverty is an advantage, facilitating his concentration, or rather, it is itself concentration, which means, of course, that he loses the advantage that lies in the application of the power of concentration."

Kafka initially formulated this note in the first person ("My spiritual poverty . . .") but later made a series of revisions that shifted it into the third person, with "A." as the object of the message. The very next entry begins with the words: "A. is laboring under the following delusion."

Kafka also used this abbreviation in Aphorisms 49 and 107.

Verschiedenheit der Anschauungen, die man etwa von einem Apfel haben kann: die Anschauung des kleinen Jungen, der den Hals strecken muss, um noch knapp den Apfel auf der Tischplatte zu sehn, und die Anschauung des Hausherrn, der den Apfel nimmt und frei dem Tischgenossen reicht.

The diversity of views that can be had of, say, an apple: the view of the little boy who has to crane his neck in order even to glimpse the apple on the table, and the view of the master of the house, who takes the apple and easily hands it to his dinner companion.

Recorded on October 22, 1917. Kafka first marked this sheet number 11; he later filled in the number 12. Here, too, it is unclear whether he had accidentally skipped over 12 in numbering the empty sheet or whether Kafka labeled a sheet "12" and later destroyed it.

The octavo notebook indicates that the example of the apple was not as randomly chosen as it might seem; there, the passage ends with the sentence: "Between the two of them is Eve." So Kafka's mind was still on the theme of Paradise (see Aphorism 3, written two days earlier).

This is an example of Kafka's pictorial thinking: although Genesis does not make explicit mention of it, Kafka visualizes Eve first *gazing up* to the forbidden fruits on the Tree of Knowledge, then plucking them and *handing* them to her companion. In other words, her "view" of the apple was first that of the little boy, then of the master of the house.

A letter to Milena Jesenská four years later laid out a similarly image-centered argument. Jesenská had evidently described the noncommittal nature of extramarital sexuality as merely "playing with a ball," and Kafka commented in assent: "It's as if Eve had picked the apple (sometimes I think I understand the Fall like no one else), but only to show it to Adam, because she liked it. Biting into it was the decisive act; playing with it wasn't allowed, but neither was it prohibited."

Ein erstes Zeichen beginnender Erkenntnis ist der Wunsch zu sterben. Dieses Leben scheint unerträglich, ein anderes unerreichbar. Man schämt sich nicht mehr, sterben zu wollen; man bittet aus der alten Zelle, die man hasst, in eine neue gebracht zu werden, die man erst hassen lernen wird. Ein Rest von Glauben wirkt dabei mit, während des Transportes werde zufällig der Herr durch den Gang kommen, den Gefangenen ansehen und sagen: "Diesen sollt Ihr nicht wieder einsperren. Er kommt zu mir."

A first indication of the onset of understanding is the wish to die. This life seems unendurable, another life unattainable. One is no longer ashamed of wishing to die; one asks to be moved from the old, hated cell to a new one, which one has yet to learn to hate. A vestige of belief is also involved in thinking that the director might happen by in the corridor, look at the prisoner, and say: "You are not to lock up this man again. He's coming to me."

Recorded on October 25 or 26, 1917.

Kafka's deviation from the semantics of everyday language is striking here: While you can *believe* that a specific thing will happen even without knowing its cause and significance, you're more likely to *hope for* a merely chance event.

This aphorism is reminiscent of a prose fragment that Kafka had recorded in his diary the previous year, where a prisoner clings to the hope that the executioner who has entered his cell will not kill him but simply bring him to a different cell.

Three months after Aphorism 13, Kafka recorded a variation on the prisoner theme in the octavo notebook: "The suicide is the prisoner who sees a gallows being erected in the prison yard, mistakenly believes it is the one intended for him, breaks out of his cell in the night and goes down and hangs himself."

In later years Kafka took the metaphor further, banishing any last ray of hope: "He could have resigned himself to a prison. To end as a prisoner—that could be a life's ambition. But it was a barred cage. Casually and imperiously, as if at home, the racket of the world streamed out and in through the bars, the prisoner was actually free, he could take part in everything, nothing that went on outside escaped him, he could even have left the cage, after all, the bars were yards apart, he was not even imprisoned." "My prison cell—my fortress." "All is imaginary—family, office, friends, the street—all imaginary, far away or close at hand, the woman closest of all, but the truth is only that you are pressing your head against the wall of a windowless and doorless cell."

14

Giengest Du über eine Ebene, hättest den guten Willen zu gehn und machtest doch Rückschritte, dann wäre es eine verzweifelte Sache; da Du aber einen steilen Abhang hinaufkletterst, so steil etwa, wie Du selbst von unten gesehen bist, können die Rückschritte auch nur durch die Bodenbeschaffenheit verursacht sein und Du musst nicht verzweifeln.

If you were walking across a plain with the best of intentions in walking onward yet were still moving backward, it would be cause for despair; but as you are clambering up a steep slope, about as steep as you yourself appear from below, moving backward can be caused only by the nature of the ground, and you needn't despair.

Recorded on November 3, 4, or 5, 1917. After Kafka copied the text onto sheet 14, he crossed it out.

Kafka indicates the autobiographical context of this text—and perhaps also the reason he crossed it out—in the very next notation in the octavo notebook: "Best of intentions? You couldn't stop your thoughts of Italy / you read P. Schlemihl aloud."

The "thoughts of Italy" probably refers to the girl he had fallen in love with in October 1913 in Riva. Kafka's diary reveals that he was still thinking about this girl in July 1916 while on vacation with Felice Bauer.

During this same stay in Marienbad, Kafka read aloud some texts to Felice, including, most likely, Adelbert von Chamisso's *Peter Schlemihl's Wondrous Story*; the engaged couple made a gift of this book to Felice's friend Grete Bloch. It is the story of a man who sells his shadow to the devil but in doing so cuts himself off from the human community.

The self-critical commentary in the octavo notebook can accordingly be understood as Kafka essentially sabotaging his romantic relationship with Felice Bauer even at the moment of their intensest closeness, preoccupied as he was with hidden erotic thoughts and with presenting Felice strategically chosen readings for them to enjoy together, readings that made her lover's ominous, self-imposed isolation painfully obvious to her. In light of the now-imminent end of his engagement, Kafka questioned whether he had always shown the "best of intentions" in moving forward with Felice.

The aphorism itself offers an additional variation on the path metaphor Kafka was so fond of using; see the commentary on Aphorism 1.

15

Wie ein Weg im Herbst: kaum ist er rein gekehrt, bedeckt er sich wieder mit den trockenen Blättern.

Like a path in autumn: no sooner has it been swept clean than it is once more covered with dry leaves.

Recorded on November 6, 1917.

Here, too, we find a variation on the path metaphor. It presumably intends to show that as time goes by, even the "true path" that has already been identified can become unrecognizable once again. At the time Kafka wrote this, he had the opportunity to experience these kinds of paths daily during his extended autumn walks in and around Zürau.

16

Ein Käfig ging einen Vogel suchen.

A cage went in search of a bird.

Recorded on November 6, 1917. In the octavo notebook, the sentence reads: "A cage went to catch a bird." The revision was made while he copied the text onto sheet 16.

The difference between the two versions is significant. At first Kafka was evidently thinking of an act of overpowering, with the cage as perpetrator and the bird as victim. Then he blurred the contours of the image: the cage will unquestionably deprive the bird of its freedom as soon as it has found it, but there is no longer any indication that it could do anything else to the bird. The cage and bird will come together. This is much closer to Kafka's view that those who lose their freedom or remain confined have invariably played a part in getting into this situation and hence also share the responsibility.

The second and final, apparently more innocuous, form of the aphorism could be projected onto any number of social relationships: a woman vying for a possible provider, a company seeking a loyal employee, et cetera. It cannot be determined from this brief text what specific kind of cage Kafka had in mind.

The question of whether the "bird" contains an allusion to Kafka's name must also remain open; see the commentary for Aphorism 32.

17

An diesem Ort war ich noch niemals: anders geht der Atem, blendender als die Sonne strahlt neben ihr ein Stern.

I have never been in this place before: breathing works differently, and a star shines next to the sun, more dazzlingly still.

Recorded on November 7 or 8, 1917.

For Kafka, the star is a metaphor not only for what is far away but also for what is radically different, in both a positive and a negative sense. Just a few weeks after writing Aphorism 17, he noted in the octavo notebook: "Anyone who believes cannot experience miracles. By day one doesn't see stars." He went on to write: "Evil is the starry sky of the Good."

Kafka also made use of this image in characterizing Kierkegaard, whose writings he studied in Zürau, in a letter to Max Brod in the spring of 1918: "the next-door neighbor has turned into some kind of star, in respect to both my admiration and a certain coldness of my sympathy." And few weeks after that, he again brought together the images of the sun and a distant place, presumably in direct reference to Aphorism 17 (though for Oskar Baum, the recipient of this letter, the reference was veiled): "Kierkegaard is a star, but one that shines over a region that is almost inaccessible to me."

In this conceptual framework, the remote region is not only a different place but also a different state of being, as indicated in Aphorism 17 by the statement that breathing "works differently" there than it does here, which refers to the effect on visitors rather than to the place itself.

In a diary entry written years later, Kafka revealed his longing for something radically different, which is the core idea of this image: "I don't want to develop in any specific manner; I want to go to a different place, it is in truth the 'desire to go to a different star.' It would be enough for me to stand right beside myself, it would be enough for me to be able to consider the place where I'm standing a different one."

18

Wenn es möglich gewesen wäre, den Turm von Babel zu erbauen, ohne ihn zu erklettern es wäre erlaubt worden.

If it had been possible to build the Tower of Babel without climbing it, that would have been allowed.

Recorded on November 9, 1917.

Kafka's impetus for this idea may have been his reading of the collection *Die Sagen der Juden* [The legends of the Jews] (1913–1927). Volume 2 of that collection states that the intention of those who built the tower was basically good, inasmuch as the tower was meant to represent the extent of divine heights; the only reprehensible part was man's endeavor to use this tower to ascend to heaven. (Volume 1 of *Die Sagen der Juden* was found in Kafka's possession.)

Three years later, Kafka wrote the prose piece "The City Coat of Arms" (title by Max Brod), a story of the failure to build the Tower of Babel, squeezed onto two printed pages.

Kafka must have regarded the tower metaphor as significant over a long period of time, since he expanded on it in several contexts. He wrote to Max Brod about a "sequence of events on one floor of the interior of the Tower of Babel, and in Babel you have no idea what is above and below." And in the fall of 1922 he wrote: "We are digging the pit of Babel."

The idea expressed in Aphorism 18 is found in Aphorism 69 as well, though not cloaked in myth.

19

Lass Dich vom Bösen nicht glauben machen, Du könntest vor ihm Geheim-nisse haben.

Don't let Evil make you believe you could keep secrets from it.

Recorded on November 10 or 11, 1917. In the octavo notebook, the sentence reads: "Don't let yourself be misled into believing you could keep secrets from Evil." He made this significant revision while copying the text onto the sheet.

The notion that Evil has a multitude of wily ways to extend its influence has often figured prominently in literature, most notably in Goethe's *Faust*.

Kafka's aphorism takes up and revises this idea to give it a sharper twist. Not only is it illusory to assume that you could conceal certain thoughts and feelings from Evil once Evil has penetrated into you, but the illusion itself stems from an insinuation on the part of Evil. Evil "knows" that you will fight off its influence, so it attempts to make you think that an unsuitable defense mechanism might be promising. Aphorism 28 resumes this idea, and Aphorism 29 widens its scope.

Aphorism 95 tells us that there are also different, surprisingly simple measures to ward off Evil.

For more on the personification of evil, see Aphorisms 7, 28, and 51 as well as the commentary on Aphorism 7. This topos also comes up in Kafka's correspondence: "I'd have given Evil his due."

20

Leoparden brechen in den Tempel ein und saufen die Opferkrüge leer; das wiederholt sich immer wieder; schliesslich kann man es vorausberechnen und es wird ein Teil der Ceremonie.

Leopards break into the temple and drink the sacrificial vessels dry; this is repeated over and over; eventually it can be calculated in advance and becomes part of the ceremony.

Recorded on November 10 or 11, 1917.

As Kafka's diary entry of June 1916 shows, he had a special interest in how religious rituals originate. At that time he was reading a newly released study, *Gudstrons uppkomst* [The origin of belief in God], by the Swedish religious scholar Nathan Söderblom, who would go on to be awarded the Nobel Peace Prize in 1930.

Kafka excerpted several historical tidbits from this book, such as the following, concerning ritual practices in a central Australian tribal culture: "Even in prehistoric times, people created totem animals in their performance of ceremonies. Thus the sacred rites themselves produced the object on which they were focused." Here, too, the rite was performed even before its object had been clearly defined. The example of the leopards, though, was most likely Kafka's own invention.

This aphorism's recourse to ethnology and its cultural and historical level of meaning set it apart from the other Zürau notes.

21

So fest wie die Hand den Stein hält. Sie hält ihn aber fest, nur um ihn desto
weiter zu verwerfen. Aber auch in jene Weite führt der Weg.

As firmly as the hand clutches the stone. But it clutches it firmly only to
fling it all the farther. Yet the path leads even into that distance.

Recorded between November 12 and 17, 1917. In the octavo notebook, Kafka changed the original "a path" to "the path."

Kafka had used the metaphor of "flinging a pebble into the world" seven years earlier in a letter to Max Brod, albeit in an altogether different context: For Brod's birthday, Kafka had sent him two books and a pebble (which is still in Brod's literary estate today) and promised to send him a pebble every year from then on.

On October 19, 1917—the same day he wrote Aphorism 1, about the "true path"—Kafka recorded in the octavo notebook: "How are you going even to touch on the greatest task . . . if you can't collect yourself so that when the decisive moment comes, you hold in your hand the entirety of yourself like a stone to be flung."

Aphorism 21 displays the emergence of a construct with entirely new contents when two previously existing metaphorically infused notions (stone-flinging and path) are joined together in a fashion that was typical for Kafka.

The revision suggests that as he wrote this aphorism, the notion of a "true path" was still on his mind; see the commentary on Aphorism 1.

22

Du bist die Aufgabe. Kein Schüler weit und breit.

You are the task. No pupil far and wide.

Recorded between November 12 and 17, 1917.

The surprising assertion "You are" in lieu of the usual "You have" is no mere hyperbole for literary effect. It has a hidden deeper meaning: If the *I* and the task are actually one and the same, the *I* would cease to exist at the moment the task is accomplished.

A letter to Max Brod, written two months *before* Aphorism 22, indicates that Kafka was aware of this consequence. In contemplating the increasingly complex existential problems they were both facing, he mused, "Misery, misery, and at the same time nothing but our own natures, and if the misery were to be disentangled at long last (perhaps only women can do such work), you and I would fall apart."

The idea that psychological conflicts and deficiencies cannot be alleviated in isolation without risking the dissolution of one's own nature also comes up frequently in his correspondence with Felice Bauer. Kafka's deep skepticism toward the therapeutic approach of psychoanalysis, which he called a "helpless mistake," also rests on this conviction.

Closely related to Aphorism 22 are an additional comment in the octavo notebook and a 1922 diary entry. In both cases, the task creates a sense of identity, yet there is no thought of a definitive solution: "The fact that our task looms just as large as our life gives it an appearance of infinity." "No one's task was as difficult, as far as I know. One might say: it is not a task, not even an impossible one, it is not even impossibility itself, it is nothing, it is not even as much of a child as the hope of a barren woman. But it is the air I breathe, as long as I go on breathing." See also Aphorism 94.

23

Vom wahren Gegner fährt grenzenloser Mut in Dich.

From the true opponent, boundless courage flows into you.

Recorded between November 12 and 17, 1917.

The "opponent" is part of the set of battle metaphors for which Kafka had a particular penchant in his letters, personal notes, and literary works. The central image of battle requires an "opponent" in order to remain coherent, but this did not stop Kafka from using the derivative metaphor in isolation. The "opponent" is consequently not a "force," however abstractly conceived, but simply whatever one has to wage battle with: adverse conditions, one's own shortcomings, evil temptations, or personal enemies.

The term "true opponent" indicates that Kafka had various levels of significance in mind, analogously to the relation between the "true path" and all other paths. The true opponent is a significant opponent, and the battle against this opponent is thus a significant and worthwhile, and hence desirable, battle.

On occasion Kafka also used these kinds of private metaphors with his friends. One example can be found in a letter to Max Brod, written a few weeks before Aphorism 23, when Brod had complained about compositional problems with his new novel, *Das grosse Wagnis* [The great risk]. Kafka tried to get across to Brod that these problems actually placed him in an enviable position: "This is a real battle, on the level of life and death, and remains so whether or not one accomplishes it. At least one has seen the opponent, or at any rate seen him flashing in the sky."

In the *Letter to His Father* (1919), Kafka makes a point of characterizing his father as a thoroughly *daunting* opponent: "Courage, determination, confidence, delight in this and that could not last all the way through when you were against it or even if your opposition could merely be assumed; and it could surely be assumed in nearly everything I did." His father was consequently, in Kafka's definition, an overpowering opponent, but not a true one—a significant distinction in his life.

24

Das Glück begreifen, dass der Boden, auf dem Du stehst, nicht grösser sein kann, als die zwei Füsse ihn bedecken.

Grasping the good fortune that the ground on which you stand cannot be larger than the two feet covering it.

Recorded between November 12 and 17, 1917.

This aphorism offers one of the examples of Kafka's willingness to go to the limit of what is grammatically possible—or even a bit beyond—for the sake of linguistic reduction. A more conventional wording—"that the ground on which you stand cannot be larger than the surface your two feet cover"—would have resulted in a doubling of metaphorical "ground" and nonmetaphorical "surface," which Kafka evidently wanted to avoid.

Kafka frequently used the word "ground" (*Boden*) in a metaphorical sense, in both the negative (run aground) and positive senses (stand on solid ground). He repeated his lament about having "no ground under his feet" for years, both to other people and in a tone of monological self-reproach.

Early on he had invoked the figure of the solitary bachelor to remark that this bachelor had "only as much ground as his two feet need," and in Zürau he observed in retrospect that it had been "the lack of ground, of air, of the commandment" that made him "fail at everything."

In a 1922 letter to Max Brod, he renewed his lament—"what weak, or rather, utterly nonexistent ground I live on"—then applied this diagnosis more broadly to the fragile existence of the writer: "A figure of this kind has no ground to stand on, has no substance, is not even made up of dust; is only the slightest bit possible in the broil of life, is only a construct of self-indulgence."

Aphorism 24 is Kafka's only known statement to go beyond this rather conventional, dull use of the ground metaphor and add a new, quasi-utopian dimension: the opportunity of standing on solid ground without the obligation, much less compulsion, to share this ground with any group.

25

Wie kann man sich über die Welt freuen, ausser wenn man zu ihr flüchtet?

How can one take pleasure in the world other than when fleeing to it?

Recorded between November 12 and 17, 1917.

The octavo notebooks often focus on connections between the world of the senses and the world of the spirit—terms that Kafka adapted from Plato's theory of forms (see Aphorisms 54, 57, 62, 85, 97). Whenever the term "world" stands alone (as in Aphorisms 41, 44, 52, 53, 60, 61, 64, 102, 103, and 105, and in the second notation on sheet 109), it is always the world of the senses that is meant.

Because there are no worlds besides these two—one of which is illusory anyhow—only an escape from the world of the spirit and the demands it poses can be meant here, an escape that inevitably and invariably leads in the direction of the world of the senses.

This aphorism appears to be quite averse to the physical world of the senses, but it should not automatically be equated with the kind of devaluation of the here and now that is inscribed in Christianity. The aim of this figure of thought is more like a temptation "to escape from the main issues . . . to the minor matters," as Kafka once wrote to Felice Bauer, an escape motivated by a feeling of being overwhelmed by the "main issues" (such as the truth of a human relationship), and it becomes possible when one experiences the more sensory "minor matters" as attractive and gratifying (by talking oneself into this perspective if necessary).

A radicalization of this idea is contained in a later note in his diary: "Escape to a conquered land and soon find it unbearable, for there is no escaping anywhere."

It is likely that this reflection was prompted by the question of Palestine, a subject of intense debate in Kafka's own milieu; but his use of the word "one" instantly shifts the message into the existential sphere, with the result that escape, *any* escape, will culminate in self-delusion.

26

Verstecke sind unzählige, Rettung nur eine, aber Möglichkeiten der Rettung wieder soviele wie Verstecke.

Es gibt ein Ziel, aber keinen Weg; was wir Weg nennen, ist Zögern.

There are countless places hiding places, only one rescue, but the possibilities for a rescue are as numerous as there are hiding places.

There is a destination but no path; what we call the path is hesitation.

The first text was recorded on November 18, 1917 (Felice Bauer's thirtieth birthday); Kafka crossed it out after copying it onto sheet 26. Kafka copied the second text from a set of later manuscript pages and added to it on the sheet. This second text originated on September 17, 1920.

Aphorism 26 is directly related to the previous one, separated in the octavo notebook only by a horizontal line. The "hiding place" is the endpoint of the "escape" into the world of the senses. The only possible rescue is to reverse the escape route and free oneself once again from the illusory nature and emptiness of the world of the senses.

But this reversal is possible from any "hiding place." Any interest that humans pursue, any activity, no matter how mundane, can become significant, from plying a trade indifferently, purely for the sake of financial gain, to throwing oneself into it wholeheartedly and aiming at perfection. Kafka's attitude on this subject, which he often expressed to others, was clearly influenced by the back-to-nature *Lebensreform* movement. "If there aren't countless opportunities for liberation," he had written to Max Brod twelve days earlier, "and especially opportunities that are there at every moment of our lives, then perhaps there are none at all."

In the second, later text, the first sentence originally read: "There is only a destination, not a path." It then became: "There is only a destination, no path." The final version did not take shape until he copied it onto the sheet.

This message is one example of Kafka's essentialist thinking. If the destination is in accordance with my nature, I already have it within me, and there is no need for a path; the only reason I am not yet "there" is that I hesitate to adhere to my nature. Here, the "true path" (see Aphorism 1) is reduced to a leap.

The concept of seamless transitions had come up two years earlier in the diary: "But questions that do not answer themselves as they emerge are never answered. There are no distances between the questioner and the responder. There are no distances to bridge. Asking and waiting therefore pointless."

27

Das Negative zu tun, ist uns noch auferlegt, das Positive ist uns schon gegeben.

Doing the negative is imposed on us; the positive is already within us.

Recorded on November 18, 19, or 20, 1917.

In a notation in the octavo notebook, which formed the basis for Aphorism 97 (see the commentary for that aphorism), Kafka explicitly calls "this world" and "the positive" opposites. The positive is ascribed to the world of the spirit—and may even be synonymous with it—while the negative is attributed to the world of the senses.

The ontological status of these two worlds differs: the world of the spirit is real and autonomous, while the world of the senses is an illusion, an artificial backdrop (see Aphorisms 54 and 62). Consequently, the positive is always "within," regardless of whether we know of or act on it, while the cheap thrills of the world of the senses demand that we become active participants.

The substantive line of demarcation between the conceptual pairs *positive/negative, good/evil,* and *spiritual/sensory* is blurry in Kafka's notes, with points of overlap. According to Aphorism 54 there is even "Evil in the spiritual realm."

28

Wenn man einmal das Böse bei sich aufgenommen hat, verlangt es nicht mehr, dass man ihm glaube.

Once you have taken Evil into yourself, it no longer insists that you believe in it.

Recorded on November 21 or 22, 1917.

This aphorism continues the idea of Aphorism 19, namely that Evil misleads the individual into making false assumptions that serve as self-justifications. Once the infection of Evil has taken hold, these self-justifications forfeit their function, and Evil ceases to care when they are maintained. This notion aligns with the psychological observation that the behavior of a person who already habitually oversteps moral bounds is no longer influenced by whether he goes on clinging to his earlier excuses and rationalizations.

For more on the personification of Evil, see Aphorisms 7, 29, and 51, and the commentary on Aphorism 7.

29

Die Hintergedanken, mit denen Du das Böse in Dir aufnimmst, sind nicht die Deinen, sondern die des Bösen.

Das Tier entwindet dem Herrn die Peitsche und peitscht sich selbst, um Herr zu werden und weiss nicht dass das nur eine Phantasie ist, erzeugt durch einen neuen Knoten im Peitschenriemen des Herrn.

The ulterior motives with which you take Evil into yourself are not your own, but those of Evil.

The animal wrests the whip from the master and whips itself in order to become the master, unaware that this is only a fantasy created by a new knot in the master's whiplash.

The first text was recorded on November 21 or 22, 1917. Kafka copied the second text from a set of later manuscript pages and added to it on the sheet. This second text was written in October 1920.

Aphorisms 19 and 39 shed light on the kind of "ulterior motives" Kafka had in mind: in one case the illusion that one could hold the damage to a minimum by keeping "secrets" from Evil, that is, sealing off a part of one's own personality from this influence; in the other the equally illusory hope that one could "pay off" the quid pro quo that Evil demands in a psychologically and socially acceptable manner. Both cases are instances of self-justifications that are actually Evil incitements. In this respect, Aphorism 29 widens the scope of Aphorisms 19 and 39.

Kafka doubted the existence of any human utterance that was devoid of ulterior motives: "At a certain state of self-knowledge . . . it is sure to happen periodically that you find yourself repugnant. . . . You will realize that you are nothing but a rat hole of wretched ulterior motives. Not the slightest action will be free of these ulterior motives."

Shortly after writing this aphorism, Kafka quoted in full the second, later text in a letter to Milena Jesenská, then noted that the behavior characterized here was "stupidity."

The image of a whip appears in a diary entry in the fall of 1916, in the context of Kafka's reading of Friedrich Wilhelm Foerster's *Jugendlehre* [Youth guidance]: "We may crack the will—that whip—over ourselves with our own hand." Aphorism 31 reveals that his skepticism toward character development based on self-mastery was still intact (see the commentary on that aphorism).

30

Das Gute ist in gewissem Sinne trostlos.

In a certain sense the Good offers no comfort.

Recorded on November 21 or 22, 1917. Kafka crossed it out after writing it on the sheet.

Two additional enties in the octavo notebook read: "Evil knows of Good, but Good does not know of Evil." "Only Evil has self-knowledge."

Good, we are told here, knows neither its counterpart nor itself. It is self-contained, static, and sealed off; in contrast to Evil, it is devoid of dynamism and any capacity for development. (The shallowness of countless morally "good" characters in literature and film is an indication of this fact.)

Consequently, the existence of Good is not necessarily comforting, in the sense of containing comfort. This layer of meaning in the aphorism emerges more conspicuously in connection with Aphorism 62, which states that the very existence of the world of the spirit robs us of hope and hence offers us no comfort.

Evil personified is devoid of comfort in yet another respect. An entry in the octavo notebook, which Kafka later crossed out, begins with the words: "The comfortless horizon of Evil, thinking his godlike status is evident in the very fact of his knowledge of Good and Evil."

31

Nach Selbstbeherrschung strebe ich nicht. Selbstbeherrschung heisst: an einer zufälligen Stelle der unendlichen Ausstrahlungen meiner geistigen Existenz wirken wollen. Muss ich aber solche Kreise um mich ziehn, dann tue ich es besser untätig im blossen Anstaunen des ungeheuerlichen Komplexes und nehme nur die Stärkung, die e contrario dieser Anblick gibt, mit nachhause.

I don't strive for self-mastery. Self-mastery means wanting to be effective at some random point within the infinite radiations of my spiritual life. But if I do have to describe such circles around myself, I had better do so inactively, merely gazing in awe at the colossal complex and taking home with me only the invigoration that this sight provides *e contrario*.

Recorded on November 23, 1917.

In August 1916, at Kafka's urging, Felice Bauer began volunteering at the Jewish Home in Berlin, which took care of Jewish refugee children from the East. The next month, the volunteers started to read Friedrich Wilhelm Foerster's *Jugendlehre* [Youth guidance, 1904], which prompted Kafka to delve into Foerster's pedagogy as well. At the core of Foerster's approach lay a well-developed conscience, self-mastery, and cultivation of an autonomous will. Kafka spotted the latent contradiction and instantly suspected that this was actually the internalization of an *external* will: "We may crack the will—that whip—over ourselves with our own hand," he commented in his diary.

Aphorism 31 shows that Kafka's skepticism of the virtue of self-mastery was ongoing. Three weeks after composing this aphorism, he wrote to Max Brod about the "pedagogy of self-mastery, which seems more and more helpless to me." Another three years later, Kafka's doubts had solidified to an outright rejection. For more on this subject, see the text expanded on sheet 29, which once again takes up the image of the whip.

Kafka presumably knew the term *argumentum e contrario* from his legal studies, where it denotes a proposition argued to be correct because it is not disproven by any case.

32

Die Krähen behaupten, eine einzige Krähe könnte den Himmel zerstören. Das ist zweifellos, beweist aber nichts gegen den Himmel, denn Himmel bedeutet eben: Unmöglichkeit von Krähen.

The crows claim that a single crow could destroy heaven. That is incontestable, but it offers no proof at all against heaven, because heaven does signify the impossibility of crows.

Recorded on November 23, 1917.

The crow is one of the many semi-private allusions Kafka liked to weave into his literary texts. Crows are close relatives of jackdaws—both belong to the corvid family—and *kavka* is the Czech word for jackdaw.

The fragments about Hunter Gracchus, which were also written in 1917, suggest that the use of this word was intended as an allusion; the Italian word *gracchio* denotes a kind of crow known as the Alpine chough (also called Gracchio alpino).

Kafka seems to have regarded the image of crows against the backdrop of a bright, clear surface as aesthetically attractive and mysteriously significant. In November 1912, when he appeared before a district court in Bohemia as a legal executive of the Workers' Accident Insurance Institute in Prague and obtained more than ten times the expected financial sum, he griped to Felice Bauer, "'You should have resisted the success,' I said to myself on the trip back when I looked at the crows over the snow-covered fields." "Swarms of crows" also circle around the tower of the castle in Kafka's novel *The Castle*.

33

Die Märtyrer unterschätzen den Leib nicht, sie lassen ihn auf dem Kreuz erhöhn, darin sind sie mit ihren Gegnern einig.

Martyrs do not underestimate the body; they let it be raised up on the cross, and in this respect they are in accord with their opponents.

Recorded on November 23, 1917. Kafka crossed it out after copying it onto the sheet.

It is striking that Kafka later cut the Christian reference for the only aphorism that contains the term *Leib* (as opposed to the more usual *Körper*) to mean "body" (see the commentary for Aphorism 102). This could be an indication of why Kafka also crossed out Aphorism 33.

Kafka rarely invoked the concept of the martyr or of martyrdom, and where he did, it was almost always in a metaphorical sense, drawn from daily life (never, however, in a political sense, as he frequently saw this term used in Jewish journalism). It is interesting to note, however, that just one day after composing Aphorism 33, he again contemplated the subject of the martyr from an ethical and epistemological perspective: "Celibacy and suicide are on a similar level of understanding, suicide and a martyr's death absolutely not, perhaps marriage and a martyr's death."

The commonality between these seemingly irreconcilable pairings lies in their ethical stance toward the world: celibacy and suicide are escape maneuvers, whereas for Kafka, marriage and a martyr's death signify an open confrontation with the highest standard.

34

Sein Ermatten ist das des Gladiators nach dem Kampf, seine Arbeit war das Weisstünchen eines Winkels in einer Beamtenstube.

His exhaustion is that of the gladiator after the battle; his work was to whitewash a corner in a clerk's office.

Recorded on November 24, 1917.

Kafka enjoyed playfully contrasting the "heroic deeds" immortalized in textbooks with equally exhausting but comparatively mundane struggles concerning marriage and professions. In a letter from Zürau, he wrote, "Knowledge on the first step. The first step of the staircase, at the top of which the marital bed is serenely set up as the reward and purpose of my human (albeit virtually Napoleonic) existence. It will not be set up, and I—it is certain—shall not get beyond Corsica."

On two occasions Kafka gave literary expression to this topos, and in both instances—as in Aphorism 34—the office is the low point that marks the extent of a character's fall. In the prose piece "The New Attorney" (1917), Alexander the Great's former battle horse serves as a modern attorney who has been admitted to the bar. In "Poseidon" (1920), the god of the sea is an ill-humored bureaucrat who sits at his desk toiling at his calculations from morning to night, and his realm appears to have dwindled to an administrative district.

In a long letter Kafka wrote in 1919 to the sister of his fiancée, Julie Wohryzek, in an attempt to justify himself, he also contrasted the militant "act" with the "office," which is ridiculous by comparison: "You who have to fight incessantly for your inner subsistence with all your might—and even that is not enough—you now want to set up a household of your own, perhaps the most necessary but surely the most affirmative and boldest act there can possibly be? What strength will you use for this? . . . exhausted by steering clear of the paltry writing in the office."

Es gibt kein Haben, nur ein Sein, nur ein nach letztem Atem, nach Ersticken verlangendes Sein.

There is no having, only a being, only a being that yearns for its last breath, for suffocation.

Recorded on November 24, 1917. In the octavo notebook, the notation first read: "There is no possession, only a being, only a being that strives for its last breath, for suffocation."

According to this statement, every form of possession is part of the world of the senses, and hence neither essential nor lasting. "Being," by contrast, is man's indestructible core, man's "truth," which is both individual and common to mankind as a whole (see Aphorism 70/71).

This declaration reflects Kafka's view that the essence of every person is immutable and that a person strives—consciously or unconsciously—to live in accordance with this essence. That is the only true "being," and at the same time it is "liberation," as defined in the octavo notebook (see the related commentary on Aphorism 37).

The death imagery Kafka invokes here does suggest, however, that "being," which belongs to the world of the spirit, has the inclination and the desire to break free of the world of the senses. In Aphorism 17 he had fantasized about a place where breathing "works differently."

One element of Kafka's psychological strategy to cope with his pulmonary tuberculosis was to shift its physical manifestations and the threats it posed to the metaphorical sphere, as well as the illness itself, which took on an increasingly symbolic significance for him. In a letter to Felix Weltsch from Zürau, written about two months after his diagnosis and five weeks before Aphorism 35, Kafka even made a point of emphasizing that for him, "suffocating," "catching breath," and even "gasping" had already become metaphors: "The village life is lovely and remains so. Ottla's house is on Ringplatz, so when I look out the window I see another cottage on the opposite side of the square, but behind that there is an open field. What could be better, in every sense, for catching my breath; as for me, I do gasp, in every sense, though least of all physically, but anywhere else I would be close to suffocating, which, however, can be withstood for years, as I know from active and passive experience."

Früher begriff ich nicht, warum ich auf meine Frage keine Antwort bekam, heute begreife ich nicht, wie ich glauben konnte fragen zu können. Aber ich glaubte ja gar nicht, ich fragte nur.

Früher begriff ich nicht,
warum ich auf meine
Frage keine Antwort be-
kam, heute begreife ich
nicht, wie ich glauben
konnte fragen zu
können.
Aber ich glaubte ja gar
nicht, ich fragte nur.

~~auf die Behauptung er
benkte zwar aber er sie
nicht. Konnte er hier
mit~~ Eine Antwort auf die
Behauptung er benkte
~~war~~ sie aber nicht, war
nur' Zittern und Glanz —

36

Früher begriff ich nicht, warum ich auf meine Frage keine Antwort bekam, heute begreife ich nicht, wie ich glauben konnte fragen zu können. Aber ich glaubte ja gar nicht, ich fragte nur.

In the past I didn't understand why I got no answer to my question; today I don't understand how I could believe I was entitled to ask. But I didn't really believe, I only asked.

Recorded on November 24, 1917. Kafka's thoughts about this aphorism appear to have occurred in two stages. In the octavo notebook, Kafka inserted a long dash before the final sentence, but he ignored it when copying the text onto the sheet.

An earlier note in Kafka's diary provides a key to understanding this aphorism. This note declares, in essence, that we ourselves are the only ones who can answer the crucial questions: "But questions that do not answer themselves as they emerge are never answered. There are no distances between the questioner and the responder. There are no distances to bridge. Asking and waiting therefore pointless."

The first phrase in the aphorism—"In the past"—may well have been meant in an autobiographical sense. Even though Kafka often diagnosed his own demise, he did concede that he had made gradual progress in attaining self-knowledge. He wrote to Oskar Baum in 1920: "In the past I always held the silly view, though it was understandable during the early years of self-medication, that on some individual occasion I was not able to recuperate properly for one reason or another, but now I know that I always carry within me this reason for not doing so."

And in the fall of 1921, when he thought about what function a future diary might have, he came to the conclusion: "I could probably write about M[ilena], but not of my own accord, and it would be aimed too squarely at myself; I no longer need to make myself as painstakingly conscious of such things as I once did, I am no longer as forgetful as I once was in this respect, I am a memory come alive, hence my insomnia."

37

Seine Antwort auf die Behauptung, er besitze vielleicht, sei aber nicht, war nur Zittern und Herzklopfen.

His response to the assertion that he might possess, but not be, was only trembling and palpitations.

Recorded on November 24, 1917. In the octavo notebook, Kafka revised "although he possesses, he is not" to read "he might possess, but not be."

At first glance, this aphorism appears to be a mere continuation of Aphorism 35, with the earlier message becoming an existential confrontation, but a semantic shift has taken place. In Aphorism 35, "being" appears as something utterly autonomous and simply a given. Aphorism 37, by contrast, suggests that it is possible to live without "being."

The contradiction is resolved in another note in the octavo notebook, written one week after Aphorism 37 (and later crossed out): "Believing means: liberating the indestructible element in oneself, or, more accurately: liberating oneself, or, more accurately: being indestructible, or, more accurately: being." Here, too, "being" is always a given because it is indestructible; even so, it must first be "liberated," which is to say, rendered conscious and be experienced, which is made possible by "believing," that is, by an unexpected and unverifiable act of faith that turns into identification (see Aphorisms 50 and 109).

This aligns with Kafka's experience—one that he lamented throughout his life and addressed in several literary texts—that a lack of identity cannot be remedied by means of arguments that lead every which way, much less by possessions, but rather by adopting a radical change of perspective and attitude toward life.

For more on the subject of "indestructibility," see Aphorisms 50, 69, 70/71.

38

Einer staunte darüber, wie leicht er den Weg der Ewigkeit ging; er raste ihn nämlich abwärts.

Someone was astonished by how easily he was moving along the path of eternity; it was because he was dashing down it.

Recorded on November 24, 1917.

Although this aphorism brings together two central concepts from the octavo notebooks—"path" and "eternity"—its meaning is not easy to reconcile with Kafka's other notes, none of which mention a "path of eternity." But there is mention of "our eternal development" (Aphorism 54) and of an "unending path"—in Aphorism 39a and elsewhere—which, Kafka tells us, leads "high in the air," just as in the fragments on Hunter Gracchus (1917), because this figure is "always on the grand staircase leading up. I clamber about on that endlessly wide open stairway, now up, now down, now right, now left, always in motion." Here, too, the possibility of downward movement is factored in.

If Kafka was thinking concretely about the path to eternal life in Aphorism 38, this path would presumably lead upward, as we can see from a note he wrote elsewhere about the Fall: "Knowledge of Good and Evil is both at the same time: a step leading up to eternal life and an obstacle to doing so." He also invoked the image of steps of knowledge leading upward in a letter from Zürau: "Knowledge on the first step. The first step of the staircase, at the top of which the marital bed is serenely set up as the reward and purpose of my human . . . existence."

In the logic of this metaphor, "dashing down" would indicate an ongoing "falling back" (a term that contains the singularly apt spatial metaphor) behind existing knowledge.

39

Dem Bösen kann man nicht in Raten zahlen—und versucht es unaufhörlich.

––––––

Es wäre denkbar dass Alexander der Grosse trotz der kriegerischen Erfolge seiner Jugend, trotz des ausgezeichneten Heeres, das er ausgebildet hatte, trotz der auf Veränderung der Welt gerichteten Kräfte die er in sich fühlte, am Hellespont stehen geblieben und ihn nie überschritten hätte undzwar nicht aus Furcht, nicht aus Unentschlossenheit, nicht aus Willensschwäche, sondern aus Erdenschwere.

It is impossible to pay Evil in installments—and one never stops trying to.

––––––

It is conceivable that Alexander the Great—despite the military successes of his youth, despite the superb army he trained, despite the powers he felt within him aimed at changing the world—might have stopped at the Hellespont and never have crossed it, not from fear, not from indecision, not from weakness of will, but from being weighed down by the force of gravity.

The first text was recorded on November 24, 1917. Kafka copied the second text from a set of later manuscript pages and added to it on the sheet. This second text was written on September 17, 1920.

The notion that one can pay Evil "in installments" is one of the illusory "ulterior motives" (denounced in Aphorism 29) that people draw on when they engage with Evil. It is the notion that one can "pay off" the quid pro quo that Evil demands in a psychologically and socially acceptable manner, that is, one can mitigate and cushion the impact of (self-)destructive consequences by restricting oneself to small doses of Evil. Ideas of this sort serve as moral self-appeasement; in Kafka's view they are not autonomous but, rather, Evil incitements (see the commentary on Aphorism 19).

For more on the personification of Evil, see Aphorisms 7, 28, 29, and 51, and the commentary on Aphorism 7.

The later text about Alexander is one of several examples of Kafka's attempts to measure himself by the destiny of historical figures. (In 1910 he had read *The Deeds of Alexander the Great*, a newly published book by Mikhail Kuzmin; see also the commentary on Aphorism 34.) In a similar vein, Kafka is said to have compared himself to Moses in a conversation with his young admirer Gustav Janouch: "I am still in Egyptian bondage. I have not yet crossed the Red Sea."

"Being weighed down by the force of gravity" means being constrained by longstanding laws and patterns of thinking and living, lacking utopian imagination, taking the view that anything radically new or different, anything thought to "cross" beyond what already exists and moves toward something unprecedented, is impossible. One entry in the octavo notebook reads: "Things that are ridiculous in the physical world are possible in the spiritual one, where there is no law of gravity . . . which we are, of course, unable to conceive of, or only when we're at a higher level."

This aphorism relates back, visually and thus notionally, to the "point" in Aphorism 5 at which there is "no turning back." In order to reach this point, a boundary must be crossed.

39a

Der Weg ist unendlich, da ist nichts abzuziehn, nichts zuzugeben und doch hält jeder noch seine eigene kindliche Elle daran. "Gewiss, auch diese Elle Wegs musst Du noch gehn, es wird Dir nicht vergessen werden."

The path is unending, nothing can be subtracted, nothing added, and yet everyone applies his own childish yardstick to it. "Certainly, you must cover this yard of the path, too, it won't be forgotten for you."

Recorded on November 25, 1917. Crossed out on the sheet.

Presumably Kafka noticed that he had inadvertently labeled two sheets "39," and therefore appended the letter "a."

It is likely that Kafka derived his notion of an "unending path," which he presented in an array of variants, from the conventional metaphor of the "path to perfection." Among the many pieces of health advice he sent to Felice Bauer—none of them meant ironically—was this one, in 1916: "Start, perhaps, by avoiding that habit of chomping on lumps of sugar; the path to the top is unending."

In a letter to Milena Jesenská written after the Zürau reflections, Kafka gave substantially more depth to this motif: "it is, of course, an insight, but only an insight along the path, and the path is unending."

For more on the path as metaphor, see Aphorisms 1, 21, 26, 38, and 104, and the commentary on Aphorism 1.

40

Nur unser Zeitbegriff lässt uns das Jüngste Gericht so nennen, eigentlich ist es ein Standrecht.

It is only our concept of time that makes us call the Last Judgment by that name; it is actually a court martial.

Recorded on November 25, 1917. Crossed out on the sheet.

If the justification of our existence is possible only within the world of the spirit—in accordance with Kafka's view (see Aphorism 99)—then the Judgment holds court in a literally timeless sphere. "This world cannot be followed by a world beyond," we read in the octavo notebook, "for the world beyond is eternal, hence it cannot have a temporal connection to this world." From a human perspective, that is, from the viewpoint of the world of the senses, it consequently appears that this court is ever present and ever active.

Here, too, Kafka is interpreting and broadening the scope of a human experience that is reflected in everyday usage in metaphorical form. When speaking about immoral or irrational decisions, people say: "It will come back to haunt you." This "it" is what appears in sublimated form as "court" in Kafka.

Eight months before writing this aphorism, Kafka had tried to give literary expression to the idea of the court martial. In a narrative fragment that was published posthumously as "The Knock at the Manor Gate," a microscopically small offense—a playful knock at a stranger's gate, or even just a hint of a knock—leads within minutes to formal court proceedings and the threat of torture.

This motif also appears in the diary. During a winter stroll at the Spindlermühle health resort in January 1922, Kafka pondered the agonizing deficiencies in his social life. He later recorded these thoughts but went on to write: "If things were only as they can seem on the path in the snow, it would be frightful; I should be lost, not in the sense of a threat but as an instantaneous execution."

41

Das Missverhältnis der Welt scheint tröstlicherweise nur ein zahlenmässiges zu sein.

It is a source of comfort that the disproportion of the world seems to be merely numerical.

Recorded on November 26, 1917. Crossed out on the sheet.

As always when Kafka uses the word "world" in his Zürau notes without further specification, he means the world of the senses, in contrast to the world of the spirit.

The "disproportion" of the world of the senses—its inescapable inadequacy—stems from its illusory, finite, and provisional nature. This deficiency is thus qualitative in nature and not merely "numerical." We can be misled by assuming that the world contains too much of this and too little of that and that a proactive rectification of this imbalance would establish order. That assumption, while comforting, is false.

In this aphorism, Kafka is reinforcing his lifelong criticism of mere "calculations" in weighing social options and consequences, although he himself had a definite proclivity for this kind of thinking (see, for example, the "summary of all the arguments for and against my marriage" that he laid out in the diary). By 1913, he was framing this criticism in the imagery that would come to characterize his writings in Zürau: "as long as you calculate, you cannot rise," which reveals that he had come up with visual representations of this perspective years earlier.

42

Den ekel- und hasserfüllten Kopf auf die Brust senken.

Lowering a head full of disgust and hatred onto one's chest.

Recorded on November 26, 1917. In the octavo notebook, the text has a sequel: "Certainly, but what if someone is throttling you?"

Gestures have a prominent role in virtually all of Kafka's literary texts, including expressive, pantomimic gestures. As is evident from several of his most noteworthy metaphors, he came across—or came up with—these gestures in a playful manner at first, and only later charged them with meaning, as was the case with the gesture of a head lowered onto a chest.

At the age of twenty-one, he visualized a pensive walk and its aftermath in terms of this gesture: "that day my head hung down so heavily that in the evening I noted in astonishment that my chin had grown into my chest." Seven years later he cited this gesture in a sober and defensive vein: "I was isolated from everyone and, faced with this story, I absolutely kept my chin pressed to my chest." The father in "The Judgment" also employs this gesture to signal the rejection of his son and the looming pivotal turn of events.

In *The Castle*, the posture of a figure on a painting acquires a positively iconographic status: "the half-length portrait of a man of about fifty. His held was bent so low on his chest that you could barely see his eyes, and the reason for this bent stance seemed to be his high, ponderous forehead and his commanding hooked nose."

For Kafka, then, lowering one's head onto one's chest goes beyond simply averting one's gaze and cutting off further communication; this gesture also signals a retreat into an interior space of reflection by turning away from the world of the senses, and indicates that the aphorism should be read as an exhortation. This conclusion is only reinforced by the second sentence in the octavo notebook.

43

Noch spielen die Jagdhunde im Hof, aber das Wild entgeht ihnen nicht, so sehr es jetzt schon durch die Wälder jagt.

The hunting dogs are still playing in the yard, but their prey will not escape them, however quickly it is already chasing through the woods.

Recorded on December 1, 1917. Kafka inadvertently dated this and other notes "November 31."

The hunt, one of Kafka's battle metaphors, had a key role in his writings. It stands for the initiative in battle, a forward movement on both sides. It is characteristic for the continuity of Kafka's thought that he employs the image in this symmetrical sense in (seemingly) innocuous letters as well as when laying out fundamental reflections.

In early 1920 he wrote to Minze Eisner, an eighteen-year-old woman with whom he was corresponding at the time: "It is good to chase one's dreams, but bad, as it mostly turns out, to be chased by them." Two years later, however, his diary said: "'Chase' is really just an image; I could also say 'onslaught against the last earthly boundary, an onslaught from below, from people, and, since this, too, is just an image, I could replace it by the image of an onslaught from above, coming down at me. The whole of this literature is an onslaught against the boundary.'"

Kafka's character Hunter Gracchus (1917) is also caught between these two forces. Although labeled a hunter, he wanders through the world "without a rudder," "always in motion," as though he himself is on the run.

In Kafka's view, this symmetry was portentous, as it is not possible to hunt without being hunted oneself, and any semblance of safety is an illusion. The hunting dogs, seemingly engaged in some other activity, are an image of this illusion and the lurking danger. This image is also found in another undated note: "The sleep of hunting dogs. They're not sleeping, just waiting for the hunt, and that looks like sleep."

See also Kafka's message to Robert Klopstock in July 1923: "any effort that lets us escape the ghosts for a moment is sweet—we almost see ourselves vanishing around the corner as they stand there stumped. Not for long, however; the hunting dogs seem to have picked up the scent already."

44

Lächerlich hast Du Dich aufgeschirrt für diese Welt.

Ludicrous, the way you have girded your loins for this world.

Recorded on December 1, 1917. For the dating of this text, see Aphorism 43.

This image, which does not come up anywhere else in Kafka's writings, appears to stem from things he observed in rural Zürau; see Aphorism 45, which immediately follows this comment in the octavo notebook. It is quite likely that Kafka, who occasionally helped out with light physical labor, could bridle a horse by himself.

"This world" means, as it always does for Kafka, the world of the senses, as opposed to the world of the spirit. Only in the illusory world of the senses is it conceivable for an attempt to use suitable prophylactic measures to prepare for an activity or long-term undertaking objectively "ludicrous," especially because the goal remains limited to the world of the senses, is thus greatly overrated in its significance, and makes the effort involved seem grotesque.

For more on the use of the word "world" without further specification, see Aphorisms 25, 41, 52, 53, 60, 61, 64, 102, 103, 105 and the second part of sheet 109.

45

Je mehr Pferde Du anspannst, desto rascher gehts—nämlich nicht das Ausreissen des Blocks aus dem Fundament, was unmöglich ist, aber das Zerreissen der Riemen und damit die leere fröhliche Fahrt.

The more horses you hitch up, the faster things go—that is, not tearing the block out of its foundations, which is impossible, but tearing apart the straps, making for a blithe and empty ride.

Recorded on December 1, 1917. For the dating of this text, see Aphorism 43.

This aphorism is closely related to the previous one, and can be read as its sequel. The two in combination offer a further example of how Kafka's ideas are guided by the ongoing potential for images and metaphors to evolve.

"Girding" and "hitching up" are followed by an attempt to undertake something impossible, using an entire team of horses. The futile attempt is not the end of the episode, however; what follows is a "blithe and empty ride," that is, a joy ride that seeks to disregard its fruitlessness. The combination of adjectives indicates that "blithe" should be understood not in the positive sense of "cheerful," but rather as a senseless, ridiculous event. And so Aphorism 45 ends like Aphorism 44; it paints a vivid picture of why the act of "girding loins" was ludicrous from the start.

It is more difficult to understand "tearing the block out of its foundations," for which Kafka offers no context in the aphorisms. But it is striking that in letters from Zürau—and nowhere else—he twice uses forms of "tearing" in a metaphorical sense. About his uncle, Siegfried Löwy, the country doctor, Kafka wrote: "he lives this way in the country, nothing tearing him away, contented." And in regard to his relationship with his father, he stated: "the roots of this antagonism cannot be torn out."

In this vein, "tearing the block out of its foundations" is used as a byword for overriding or radically altering a condition that is fundamentally unalterable, with the "blithe and empty ride" a childish simulation of success.

46

Das Wort "sein" bedeutet im Deutschen beides: Da-sein und Ihm-gehören.

In German, the word *sein* means both "being" and "belonging to him."

Recorded on December 1, 1917. For the dating of this aphorism, see Aphorism 43.

Earlier that day, Kafka had tried to formulate this idea in the octavo notebook: "In German, 'being' and 'belonging to him' are designated in the same way, with *sein*." He crossed out this sentence.

This first wording is misleading in the context of the aphorisms, because for Kafka, the natural "being" (*Dasein*) that inheres in every living creature is something distinct from *sein*; in fact, Aphorisms 35 and 37 even imply that there could be life without *sein*, namely a life that is limited to the will to possess (see Aphorism 57). For Kafka, *sein* always means a life that lays open and unfolds one's own essence. But because this essence is indestructible and is therefore part of a world that crosses over to and encompasses our world of the senses, *sein*, in the emphatic sense, means belonging to that all-encompassing "world of the spirit," with no clear dividing line between the terms "spiritual" and "divine." The aphorism asserts that in German this state of affairs is revealed in the language itself.

Kafka's stance on marriage offers a concrete example of partaking in a higher order. In his view, a marriage that arises from the innermost necessity and is sustained by the deepest understanding—and only this kind—leads up to a higher level; it even clears the way to an otherwise unattainable absolute. He noted in his diary: "As insignificant as I may be, no one is here who has understanding for me as a whole. To have someone who possesses this understanding, such as a wife, would mean having support on every side, having God." The converse, which he discovered in the Talmud, "A man without a wife is not a person," made perfect sense to Kafka. This substantialist view of marriage even led him to defend the small-minded conventions of his prospective mother-in-law: "she is right, after all—and to quite some degree!—in thinking that any way of life other than marriage between a man and a woman is pointless."

47

Es wurde ihnen die Wahl gestellt Könige oder der Könige Kuriere zu werden. Nach Art der Kinder wollten alle Kuriere sein. Deshalb gibt es lauter Kuriere, sie jagen durch die Welt und rufen, da es keine Könige gibt, einander selbst die sinnlos gewordenen Meldungen zu. Gerne würden sie ihrem elenden Leben ein Ende machen, aber sie wagen es nicht wegen des Diensteides.

They were offered the choice between becoming kings or the couriers of kings. In the manner of children, they all wanted to be couriers. And so there are only couriers. They rush through the world and, as there are no kings, they shout their now-meaningless messages to one another. They would gladly put an end to their wretched lives, but don't dare to because of their oaths of service.

Recorded on December 2, 1917.

This aphorism depicts a characteristic paradox in Kafka's writings: There is not too *little* information ("messages") but too *much*. Since no single piece of information is authenticated, however, the informative value remains virtually nil.

This same perspective, also in aphoristic form, is found in Kafka's prose piece "The New Attorney" (1917): "no one points out the direction; many carry swords, but only to brandish them, and the gaze that tries to follow them gets confused." Although we are told that this was different in earlier times, it is doubtful that Kafka had a critique of his era in mind.

The Trial and *The Castle* also contain a plethora of informational tidbits that consistently prove hollow and can never be traced back to a specific initiator; this coupling of information with a lack of informative value functions as a central motif in guiding the plots of these novels. As we see in his often humorous scenes, Kafka had a predilection for portraying communication failures: in *The Trial* there are professional "information officers" whose statements are limited to information about themselves, and in *The Castle* useful information is passed along only when it has been determined that the addressee is sleeping.

Furthermore, the aphorism suggests the power of a higher authority, the name or image of which, however, is consistently omitted. It is not stated who asked the couriers about their career aspirations ("They were offered the choice"), or who required them to swear an "oath of service." This, too, is a literary technique that Kafka frequently invoked in his novels.

48

An Fortschritt glauben heisst nicht glauben, dass ein Fortschritt schon geschehen ist. Das wäre kein Glauben.

Belief in progress doesn't mean belief that progress has already been made. That would not be belief.

Recorded on December 4 or 5, 1917.

In the Zürau notes, Kafka always uses the term "belief" in an emphatic sense, that is, in the sense of an identification with the object of that belief and not merely as acceptance of a fact (on this distinction, see also Aphorism 100).

Progress can be verified, provided that there are clearly specified criteria for what we understand by progress. A belief that progress has been made would therefore be a mere belief in facts, which can fundamentally carry over into knowledge.

A passage in Kafka's story "Investigations of a Dog" (1922) illustrates the difference: "People often sing the praises of the overall progress of dogdom through the ages, and the main thing they seem to have in mind is the progress of science. Certainly science marches on—that is unstoppable—it even marches on at an accelerating speed, faster and faster, but what is there to praise in this? It is as if someone wanted to praise a person for growing older as the years go by and as a result death approaches ever more rapidly. This is a natural and, furthermore, an ugly process, and one in which I find nothing to praise. I see only decline. . . ." This narrator clearly accepts progress as a fact but does not "believe" in progress.

49

A. ist ein Virtuose und der Himmel ist sein Zeuge.

A. is a virtuoso and heaven is his witness.

Recorded on December 4 or 5, 1917.

This aphorism can be read in two ways. One is as irony, in the sense that A. claims to be a virtuoso, but the only indication of his lofty status is a reference to a mysterious higher realm. This is the exact situation in Kafka's last short story, "Josefine the Singer, or the Mouse Folk." Josefine, who in truth can barely manage to get out a mouse's "perfectly ordinary whistling," maintains that she is a singer and hence an artist, but an artist who "in her opinion sings to deaf ears" and therefore lays claim to legitimacy not from the social community but from the sphere of art itself.

A second, irony-free way of reading this aphorism would be that true virtuosity always relies on a special connection to the "world of the spirit," much the way we might speak of a "gifted artist" whose giftedness is not affirmed by an audience. An artist of this kind would be truly independent of audience affirmation and justified in invoking higher authorities.

Evidence for the ironic interpretation is that the Zürau octavo notebooks always use the abbreviation "A." for a "someone" who is clearly laboring under a delusion. But as we often see in Kafka's letters and diaries, he was able to adopt both perspectives: that of the absolute claim to artistic status and the ironic view by the active community of the requirements of art, which are difficult to endorse, let alone cash in on.

For more on the abbreviation "A.," see the commentary on Aphorism 10.

50

Der Mensch kann nicht leben ohne ein dauerndes Vertrauen zu etwas Unzerstörbarem in sich, wobei sowohl das Unzerstörbare als auch das Vertrauen ihm dauernd verborgen bleiben können. Eine der Ausdrucksmöglichkeiten dieses Verborgen-Bleibens ist der Glaube an einen persönlichen Gott.

Man cannot live without an enduring trust in something indestructible within him, though both the indestructible element and the trust may remain forever hidden from him. One of the ways of expressing this abiding hiddenness is the belief in a personal god.

Recorded on December 7, 1917. It was only after copying the text onto the sheet that Kafka specified the wording of "trust in something indestructible" to have it read "trust in something indestructible within him." After adding these words, however, he crossed out the entire aphorism.

It is obvious that this aphorism did not become conceptually consistent until the final revision on the sheet. "Trust in something indestructible" outside of oneself could also be a belief in God, which would render the second sentence of the aphorism superfluous.

The term "trust" does not appear anywhere else in the Zürau octavo notebooks. Here Kafka may be using it in the sense of "belief" solely to avoid word repetition. Aphorism 109 illustrates the way that this fundamental a belief can become operative while remaining inadvertent.

The fact that Kafka characterizes faith in God as a mere "expression" of a different belief that remains hidden makes it unlikely that he himself believed in a personal god. Even so, he used the word "divine" synonymously with "indestructible"; see the commentary on Aphorism 69.

Kafka presumably came upon the concept of indestructibility in Schopenhauer, whose writings he had first studied in detail during the previous year. Chapter 41 in volume 2 of Schopenhauer's *The World as Will and Representation* bears the title: "On Death and Its Relation to the Indestructibility of Our Inner Nature." For Schopenhauer, as for Kafka, this indestructibility is both extratemporal and unaware of its own existence, but for very different reasons: Schopenhauer does not identify it as something spiritual or psychological, let alone as an individual attribute, but rather as the eternal, vital principle of the "will," which in his view lies at the core of all material and spiritual phenomena.

For more on the "indestructible," see Aphorism 70/71 and the commentary on Aphorism 37.

51

Es bedurfte der Vermittlung der Schlange: das Böse kann den Menschen verführen, aber nicht Mensch werden.

The mediation of the serpent was essential: Evil can seduce man but not become man.

Recorded on December 7, 1917. The octavo notebook version first read: "Evil can speak to man. . . ." Kafka made the revision before copying it onto the sheet, then he crossed it out.

The Old Testament's Paradise myth frequently appears in the Zürau octavo notebooks (see Aphorisms 64, 74, 82, and 84 and the commentary on Aphorism 3), along with the serpent as a mouthpiece and agent of Evil: "Adam's first house pet after the expulsion from Paradise was the serpent." "According to God, the immediate consequence of eating of the Tree of Knowledge was to be death; according to the serpent (or at least it could be understood this way), becoming like God. Both were wrong in similar ways." "The serpent did its work only halfway in giving its advice, now it also has to try falsifying what it has brought about, namely to bite its own tail in the true sense."

But Kafka also used the image in an extended metaphorical context: "'Know thyself' does not mean 'Scrutinize thyself.' 'Scrutinize thyself' is what the serpent says."

In Kafka's view, Evil assuming a human form—after which there would be no more need for the serpent—is bound to fail because of the "indestructible" core of man and mankind, for if this were to happen, Evil would be allotted part of the "divine." Seen from an even higher, ontological observation point, this argument also falls apart, however, because if there is essentially nothing but a world of the spirit, Evil must be also contained within it in some form or another; see Aphorism 54.

For more on the limits of Evil, see Aphorism 95.

52

Im Kampf zwischen Dir und der Welt sekundiere der Welt.

In the battle between yourself and the world, act as second to the world.

Recorded on December 8, 1917. Kafka crossed it out after copying it.

This aphorism is closely related to the following one, 53, which was written on the same day. The two aphorisms make a comparable demand, but the demand in Aphorism 52 goes significantly further, as it requires not only fairness but also active support of the opponent. It would appear that Kafka was concerned about the overly conspicuous thematic overlap and duplication, so he opted to cross out the starker demand.

This aphorism refers to the world of the senses (as is always the case when the world of the spirit is not designated explicitly). In the epistemological sense, Kafka considers this world illusory and hence subordinate, but the categorization does not apply to its ethical status. Kafka was not drawn to escapism, nor did he express contempt for the world. On the contrary, numerous statements in his diaries and letters attest to his admiration for anyone who lends credence to the Good within *this* world by performing acts of charity, engaging in a profession aimed at bettering society, or taking on the responsibility of a family. The substance of this aphorism is thus an altogether practical one: If the world places these kinds of demands on you, yield to them, no matter how hard they may be.

For Kafka, this principle did not apply to literature, which has its own claim to truth, and he believed that pursuing literature necessitated turning his back on the world of the senses: "All of this literature is an onslaught against the boundary. . . ." Throughout his life, he regarded the conflict between the tangible claims of the world and the claims of literature, which went well beyond those, as a "battle."

53

Man darf niemanden betrügen, auch nicht die Welt um ihren Sieg.

One must not cheat anyone, not even the world of its victory.

Recorded on December 8, 1917.

This aphorism is a toned-down version of Aphorism 52, which was written on the same day (and later crossed out). Here we are asked only to acknowledge candidly our own inferiority once it becomes clear that we are unequal to the challenges posed by the world of the senses, and we cannot successfully counter it with our own non-sensory, "spiritual" challenges.

This reflection is related to musings on his own life story, which Kafka stepped up after the onset of tuberculosis, especially in Zürau. Three weeks earlier, he had written to Max Brod: "In the city, family, profession, society, love relationships (you can put that first, if you like), the existing or prospective community at large: in all these relationships I have not stood the test, and moreover have failed to do so in such a way that—I have observed this carefully—no one else anywhere around me has." Kafka continued his letter by claiming that he had discovered a surprising way out: "It amounts to, or would amount to, my confessing not only in private, not only as an aside, but openly, by my behavior, that I cannot acquit myself properly here. To this end, I need do nothing but follow the contours of my previous life with full determination. As a result I would hold myself together, not squander myself in meaninglessness, and maintain a clear-eyed view."

This autobiographical context makes it unlikely that in writing Aphorisms 52 and 53 Kafka was thinking of an inevitable, preordained victory of the world that applies to every individual case. The second text on sheet 54 also speaks against a generalization of this kind.

54

Es gibt nichts anderes als eine geistige Welt; was wir sinnliche Welt nennen ist das Böse in der geistigen und was wir böse nennen ist nur eine Notwendigkeit eines Augenblicks unserer ewigen Entwicklung.

Mit stärkstem Licht kann man die Welt auflösen. Vor schwachen Augen wird sie fest, vor noch schwächeren bekommt sie Fäuste, vor noch schwächeren wird sie schamhaft und zerschmettert den, der sie anzuschauen wagt.

There is nothing other than a world of the spirit; what we call the world of the senses is the Evil in the spiritual realm, and what we call Evil is only a momentary necessity in our eternal development.

With the very strongest light, one can dissolve the world. Before weak eyes it becomes solid, before even weaker eyes it acquires fists, before eyes that are weaker still it grows abashed and smashes anyone who dares to gaze upon it.

This aphorism was recorded on December 8, 1917, through "the Evil in the spiritual realm"; the rest was added when he copied the text onto the sheet. In the octavo notebook, Kafka initially miswrote: "There is only a world of the senses...."

Kafka copied the second text from a set of later notations. It originally read "Before small eyes" instead of "Before weak eyes." This second text was written in October or November 1920.

Aphorism 54 assumes a central significance in the set because the first clause contains an ontological statement that provides the key to understanding many of the other aphorisms (notably, Aphorisms 25, 41, 44, 57, 60, 62, 85, 97, 105). Kafka takes the primacy of the world of the spirit as a starting point in assigning a lesser ontological status to Evil, which is illusory and fleeting, like the world of the senses as a whole. At the same time, however, he declares Evil an essential transitional phenomenon. This aphorism is also Kafka's attempt to coalesce the epistemological distinction between *spirit/senses* and the moral distinction between *good/evil* on an ontological level.

For more on the question of Evil, see Aphorisms 19, 28, 29, 39, 51, 55, 85, 86, 95, 100, and 105, and the commentary on Aphorism 7. For additional remarks on "eternal development," see the commentary on Aphorism 38.

Regarding the second text, the terms "light," "eyes," and "gaze" indicate that the focus here is not a practical confrontation with the world but rather the process of gaining insight into it. The terms "fists" and "smashes," by contrast, signal that this process is also part of the "battle between yourself and the world," as addressed in Aphorisms 52 and 53. In this sense, "dissolv[ing]" the world signifies recognizing its illusory character, while the weakest eyes have no notion whatever of this illusory nature, and so the world becomes an *absolute* threat for them.

Kafka's belated decision to group this text with the Zürau aphorisms underscores the fact that this is a meta-reflection, as those aphorisms were themselves an attempt to produce the "strongest light."

55

Alles ist Betrug: das Mindestmass der Täuschungen suchen, im üblichen bleiben, das Höchstmass suchen. Im ersten Fall betrügt man das Gute, indem man sich dessen Erwerbung zu leicht machen will, das Böse, indem man ihm allzu ungünstige Kampfbedingungen setzt. Im zweiten Fall betrügt man das Gute, indem man also nicht einmal im Irdischen nach ihm strebt. Im dritten Fall betrügt man das Gute, indem man sich möglichst weit von ihm entfernt, das Böse, indem man hofft, durch seine Höchststeigerung es machtlos zu machen. Vorzuziehen wäre also hiernach der zweite Fall, denn das Gute betrügt man immer, das Böse in diesem Fall, wenigstens dem Anschein nach, nicht.

Everything is cheating: whether seeking the minimum of deceptions, staying within the usual level, or seeking the maximum. In the first case one cheats the Good by making it too easy to acquire, and the Evil by setting overly unfavorable combat conditions. In the second case one cheats the Good by not striving for it, even in earthly terms. In the third case one cheats the Good by creating the greatest possible distance from it, and the Evil by maximizing it in the hope of rendering it powerless. Accordingly, then, the second case is preferable, for one always cheats the Good, but in this case, or so it would at least appear, not the Evil.

Recorded on December 8, 1917.

This aphorism is the attempt to examine two types of human battles—the epistemological battle for truth and the moral battle for Good—in their mutual intertwinement.

The first option Kafka sets forth states that one can make it easier to "acquire" the Good, that is, *become* good, by getting as close to the truth as possible beforehand, thus robbing Evil of its most potent weapon—deception—and the path to Good will lie open.

This is "cheating" insofar as it amounts to an impermissible change of battleground. Kafka insists that in order to become good, one must actually tackle certain moral conflicts successfully and not simply skirt them by intellectual means (that is, by engaging in deception and thus rendering superfluous the true, moral battle).

This concept also forms the backdrop to Aphorisms 52 and 53, and explains Kafka's skepticism regarding a victory at any cost.

The two other options can be regarded analogously. The seemingly bizarre idea that one could render Evil powerless by going along with all its attempts at cheating, feigning stupidity, can also be understood in this vein. The hope would be that a victory of Evil could have little effect in this instance, since the victory would have already occurred in the intellectual realm, before the onset of the moral confrontation. Here, too, the "cheating" would consist of switching the battleground in time.

56

Es gibt Fragen, über die wir nicht hinwegkommen könnten, wenn wir nicht von Natur aus von ihnen befreit wären.

There are questions we could not get past if we were not freed of them by nature.

Recorded on December 8, 1917. Kafka had already substituted "we" for "one" in the octavo notebook.

The context of the octavo notebook does not indicate what kinds of questions Kafka had in mind here. The phrase "by nature," which does not appear in any of his other writings, would appear to indicate that he is thinking not of limits to the reflective faculty but of physiological or biological restrictions, and those that apply not only to the individual but to human beings as a whole, as the word "we" underscores.

Many of the ethical questions regarding human reproduction and mortality that we grapple with today were barely relevant in Kafka's lifetime. Even though these questions could have been posed, they would not have given rise to the ethical dilemmas we now face, as the absence of the requisite technology did not allow for any natural means of intervention, and so society would "get past" them.

57

Die Sprache kann für alles ausserhalb der sinnlichen Welt nur andeutungs-weise, aber niemals auch nur annähernd vergleichsweise gebraucht werden, da sie entsprechend der sinnlichen Welt nur vom Besitz und seinen Beziehungen handelt.

For everything outside the world of the senses, language can be used only by way of suggestion, but can never even come close to being used representationally because it is concerned only with possession and its associations, in accordance with the world of the senses.

Recorded on December 8, 1917.

According to this aphorism, language is based in the "world of the senses," and hence its scope is limited to fleeting, relative phenomena, while the world of the spirit, as a source of truth, is fundamentally closed off to it. In this view, even the most sophisticated literature has no access to the truth; it can at best "suggest" (such as with enigmatic images, as Kafka himself does). An adequate, accurate suggestion can be recognized as such when—as Aphorism 63 tells us—it radiates and truly captures something of the light of truth.

It follows that truth itself, as a spiritual entity, has no need to be expressed in language: "Muteness is an attribute of perfection," Kafka recorded in the octavo notebook. According to Aphorism 80, truth is also incapable of self-reflection.

For Kafka, an essential difference between the world of the senses and the world of the spirit is that only the world of the spirit can have an actual *being*, while the world of the senses cannot get beyond *having* and possessing, in the sense of illusory connections that form no more than fleeting identities. This explains his view that language, too, is necessarily restricted to the level of *having*, while *being* remains out of reach.

Aphorism 57 is a meta-reflection in that it relegates language itself—and hence all the aphorisms language can form—to narrow confines of knowledge. Accordingly, this aphorism, too, relies on suggestion, thus justifying Kafka's formal experiments with the literary genre of the aphorism.

On the connections between the world of the senses and the world of the spirit, see also Aphorisms 54, 62, 85, and 97.

58

Man lügt möglichst wenig nur, wenn man möglichst wenig lügt, nicht wenn man möglichst wenig Gelegenheit dazu hat.

The way to lie as little as possible is only by lying as little as possible, not by having the least possible opportunity to do so.

Recorded on December 8, 1917. In the octavo notebook, the aphorism initially read: "The way to lie as little as possible is only by lying as little as possible, not be speaking as little as possible." This revision clearly served to encompass additional forms of lying, such as written or gestural lies. Kafka crossed out the note on sheet 58.

This sentence is related to Aphorism 55, which also concerns options for using careful reflection to steer clear of the need to uphold one's moral worth; these options are characterized as "cheating."

As applied to lies, it would not constitute moral progress merely to ensure that one has as little opportunity as possible to lie—by staying silent, for example—because this trick would improperly shift the battleground, and the confrontation with Evil would no longer take place in a moral arena but rather in an intellectual one.

For Kafka this was no abstract reflection. He had long entertained the notion that lies can be curtailed not only by means of honesty but also by noncommunication. Back in 1913, he had written in his diary: "Within myself, devoid of a human relationship, there are no visible lies. The limited circle is pure."

He became increasingly insistent on this point, in the Zürau reflections as well. He had even had disputes with Milena Jesenská over the issue, because in spite of her urgent plea he could not even bring himself to tell a white lie that would have enabled them to meet. He wrote to her in 1920: "And now I'll keep my mouth shut in order to stick with the truth just a little. Lying is appalling; there's no worse mental agony."

For more on the contrastive pair of *lie/truth*, see Aphorism 80.

59

Eine durch Schritte nicht tief ausgehöhlte Treppenstufe ist, von sich selbst aus gesehn, nur etwas öde zusammengefügtes Hölzernes.

A stair not deeply hollowed out by footsteps is, from its own point of view, merely a lackluster assemblage of wood.

Recorded on December 9 or 10, 1917. The octavo notebook says "a special assemblage of wood." The change was made when Kafka copied it onto the sheet, after which he crossed out the aphorism.

The stair that is not deeply hollowed out is an object whose intended use has yet to leave its mark, and appears to be functional only in context—for instance in the case of a newly constructed building—but not in and of itself, much less "from its own point of view."

This latter wording, which attributes consciousness to the object in somewhat the form of a thought experiment, makes it clear that the usage is symbolic. Even a person with well-defined talents and capabilities, which for whatever reason go unused—especially by other people—and therefore fail to leave any physiognomic traces won't make for an interesting character, either from the outside or the inside.

60

Wer der Welt entsagt, muss alle Menschen lieben, denn er entsagt auch ihrer Welt. Er beginnt daher das wahre menschliche Wesen zu ahnen, das nicht anders als geliebt werden kann, vorausgesetzt dass man ihm ebenbürtig ist.

Whoever renounces the world must love all people, for he is also renouncing their world. He thus begins to gain a sense of the true nature of man, which cannot be anything other than loved, assuming that one is its equal.

Recorded on December 9 or 10, 1917. Kafka subsequently placed quotation marks around "world" in the clause "for he is also renouncing their world." The sheet, however, does not retain these quotation marks.

For Kafka, "renouncing the world" means forgoing any interest in relationships—in the world of the senses—that are based solely on possessions (see Aphorisms 35 and 57). Although I may initially do this for myself, I quickly lose interest in all others' relationships that are based on possessions.

Only then is it possible to divine the "true nature of man," man's "indestructible" element that lies beyond these illusory relationships. This "indestructible" element—as Aphorisms 50 and 70/71 tell us—is common to all people and hence creates a "supremely indivisible connection." This connection is ever present on an unconscious level, but it can—as stated in Aphorism 60—also become conscious, as love.

The concluding words declare that is not only sufficient but essential to renounce the world of the senses in order to attain human love. Only this renunciation renders us "equal" to that indestructible nature, even if we are unable to recognize it. For the consequences of this reflection, see the following aphorism, 61.

61

Wer innerhalb der Welt seinen Nächsten liebt tut nicht mehr und nicht weniger Unrecht als wer innerhalb der Welt sich selbst liebt. Es bliebe nur die Frage, ob das erstere möglich ist.

Whoever in this world loves his neighbor does neither more nor less wrong than whoever in this world loves himself. The only remaining question is whether the former is possible.

Recorded on December 9 or 10, 1917. Kafka crossed it out after copying it onto the sheet.

This aphorism is the conceptual sequel to Aphorism 60 and can only be understood as such. (The two texts appear on the same page of the octavo notebook.) Kafka was evidently attempting to counter the objection that love between people is also possible "in this world," that is, within the world *of the senses*.

Not daring to deny that, he left the question open. Aphorism 61 is a rare instance of Kafka's hesitation to see an idea through to its logical conclusion. Still, he diminishes the value of loving one's neighbor in a manner that goes against any notions of social ethics: If I love another person, complete with all the illusory, sensual, possession-based relationships in which the person is enmeshed, this love is no higher, "neither more nor less wrong," than my love of myself and *my* possessions. These two paths miss out in equal measure on the "true nature of man" as put forth in Aphorism 60.

The context in the octavo notebook shows that Kafka's thinking was still in flux here. Aphorisms 60 and 61 appear to be embedded in a reflection that brings a related concept, the "soul," into play: "The observer of the soul cannot penetrate into the soul, but there is still a marginal line at which he comes into contact with it. The fact that even the soul does not know of itself shows a recognition of this contact. It must therefore remain unknown. [This is where Aphorism 60 follows, between two horizontal lines.] That would be sad only if there were anything besides the soul, but there is nothing else."

Hence it follows that the soul also belongs to the "world of the spirit" (see Aphorism 62), as do the equally elusive "nature of man" and the "indestructible." This notation indirectly confirms that love is founded on no more than an inkling of those spiritual entities, and not on actual knowledge of them.

62

Die Tatsache, dass es nichts anderes gibt als eine geistige Welt, nimmt uns die Hoffnung und gibt uns die Gewissheit.

The fact that there is nothing but a world of the spirit takes away our hope and gives us certainty.

Recorded on December 9 or 10, 1917.

This aphorism starts by repeating the core message of Aphorism 54, then proceeds to draw a conclusion from what was said there about the relationship between the world of the senses and that of the spirit.

If the world of the senses is actually nothing but "Evil in the spiritual realm," any hope of attaining something like redemption or liberation within this world is dashed, regardless of how we try to do so, whether by means of art, or by engaging in practical activities, or by becoming part of a community. In 1920 Kafka said to Brod, half-jokingly, that there was hope only for God but not for us.

If, on the other hand, as Aphorism 54 says, Evil is "only a momentary necessity in our eternal development," we can at least rest assured that we won't stay confined within the limits of the world of the senses forever, even though it is by no means certain that this "eternal development" necessarily leads upward (see Aphorism 38).

63

Unsere Kunst ist ein von der Wahrheit Geblendet-Sein: Das Licht auf dem zurückweichenden Fratzengesicht ist wahr, sonst nichts.

Our art is one of being bedazzled by truth: The light cast on the recoiling, contorted face is true, and nothing else is.

Recorded on December 11, 1917. Kafka changed "art" to "our art" when he wrote the text on the sheet.

In Aphorism 57, Kafka used the example of literature to establish that art itself has no direct access to the truth but can at best capture emanations of truth (see the commentary there). Kafka's writings contain no analogous reflections on the nonlinguistic arts, yet the generalization in Aphorism 63 shows that Kafka also confines music and painting to the world of the senses.

About six weeks later he noted in the octavo notebook: "Art flies around the truth, but with the firm intention of not getting burned. Its ability lies in finding, in the dark void, a place where the beam of light can be intercepted forcefully without having been perceptible before."

The reason that the bedazzled "contorted face" has to recoil from the truth is also stated in the added text on sheet 106, namely that we cannot bear the sight of unvarnished truth, and direct confrontation with it would turn us "into a pillar of salt."

In a letter written in the final year of his life, Kafka indicated that he no longer saw the potential of art in such restricted terms, since it did enhance human communication, more so than conversations and letters: "Sometimes the nature of art as a whole, the existence of art, strikes me as explicable only in terms of such 'strategic considerations,' allowing for the exchange of truthful words from person to person."

64

*Die Vertreibung aus dem Paradies ist in ihrem Hauptteil ewig: Es ist
also zwar die Vertreibung aus dem Paradies endgültig, das Leben in der
Welt unausweichlich, die Ewigkeit des Vorganges aber macht es trotzdem
möglich, dass wir nicht nur dauernd im Paradiese bleiben könnten, sondern
tatsächlich dort dauernd sind, gleichgültig ob wir es hier wissen oder nicht.*

The expulsion from Paradise is in its principal aspect eternal: and so, although the expulsion from Paradise is definitive, and life in the world
inescapable, the very eternity of the process nevertheless makes it possible
not only that we could remain in Paradise forever but that we are indeed
there forever, whether we know it here or not.

Recorded on December 12, 1917. In the octavo notebook, the first sentence reads: "The expulsion from Paradise is in its principal aspect an extratemporal, eternal process." After copying the text onto the sheet, Kafka made an additional revision. It initially read: ". . . but the very eternity of the process, or, to put it in temporal terms, the eternal repetition of the process nevertheless makes it possible. . . ."

In both revisions Kafka took back any explicit reference to the nontemporality of this process. Kafka continued this sort of revision in the very next entry in the octavo notebook, which states: "Every moment also corresponds to something extratemporal. This world cannot be followed by a world beyond, for the world beyond is eternal, hence it cannot have a temporal connection to this world." Kafka crossed out the first sentence of this note, again removing the word "extratemporal."

This note offers a key to understanding the aphorism, as its message can also be inverted. Because there can be no temporal connection between this world and the world beyond, the world beyond cannot *precede* this world, which means that outside of our limited concept of time the process of expulsion goes on, and hence our existence in Paradise itself.

Kafka was attempting to reconcile the mythical process of the expulsion—the descent to "this world," to the "earth," to the "world of the senses"—with his view that the essence of man is indestructible in his core, whether man is aware of it or not (see Aphorisms 50, 69, 70/71). Consequently, man remains at home in both spheres, and retains some share of "eternity"; the process of expulsion does not come to a close.

Aphorism 66, immediately following this one, continues this idea of a dual affiliation.

For more on the motif of the expulsion from Paradise, see the commentary on Aphorism 3.

66

Er ist ein freier und gesicherter Bürger der Erde, denn er ist an eine Kette gelegt, die lang genug ist, um ihm alle irdischen Räume frei zu geben und doch nur so lang, dass nichts ihn über die Grenzen der Erde reissen kann. Gleichzeitig aber ist er auch ein freier und gesicherter Bürger des Himmels, denn er ist auch an eine ähnlich berechnete Himmelskette gelegt. Will er nun auf die Erde drosselt ihn das Halsband des Himmels, will er in den Himmel jenes der Erde. Und trotzdem hat er alle Möglichkeiten und fühlt es, ja er weigert sich sogar das Ganze auf einen Fehler bei der ersten Fesselung zurückzuführen.

He is a free and secure citizen of the earth, for he is attached to a chain long enough to give him access to all parts of the earth, and yet only so long that nothing can pull him over the edges of the earth. At the same time, however, he is also a free and secure citizen of heaven, for he is also attached to a heavenly chain with similar dimensions. If he wants to go to earth, the heavenly collar will choke him, if he wants to go to heaven, the earthly collar will. Yet even so, all possibilities are open to him, and he feels this; indeed, he even refuses to ascribe the whole thing to an error in the original enchainment.

Recorded on December 14, 1917. There is no record of a sheet numbered 65. If this sheet ever existed, only two notations could have been intended for it, either the note about the connection between this world and the world beyond (see the commentary on sheet 64) or the succeeding sentence in the octavo notebook, dated December 13: "He who seeks does not find; he who does not seek is found."

In the previous aphorism, 64, Kafka explained why man's dual affiliation to earth and heaven remains intact in spite of the expulsion from Paradise. Aphorism 66 draws a far-reaching conclusion in stating that a deliberate and enduring passage from heaven to earth (that is, from the world of the spirit to the world of the senses) is as impossible as the other way around.

The reason that man nevertheless has "all possibilities" open to him is that the two worlds have a dissimilar ontological status, and hence no actual boundary exists between them. The earthbound world of the senses is illusory, while the celestial world of the spirit is absolute—which is why Aphorism 62 can claim that there is nothing *but* a world of the spirit.

This lack of conceptual clarity and these apparent contradictions result from Kafka's allowing for both an ontological and an anthropological perspective rather than opting for one over the other. From an ontological view, we were not really "expelled," because there is no "place" beyond the world of the spirit. From an anthropological perspective, an expulsion from heaven really did take place, but because Kafka had to bear his ontological interpretation in mind, he described this expulsion in a substantially more complex manner than the monotheistic religions did.

67

Er läuft den Tatsachen nach wie ein Anfänger im Schlittschuhlaufen, der überdies irgendwo übt, wo es verboten ist.

He runs after the facts like a novice skater who also practices someplace where it is forbidden.

Recorded on December 17 or 18, 1917.

Kafka often felt that in his outer life he was confronting the onslaught of the "facts" quite ineptly, that he was grasping them far too slowly, assessing them incorrectly, placing them in false contexts, and learning nothing from them, which meant that each new fact caught him unawares.

"I have no memory," he wrote to Felice Bauer, "not for things I've learned, or read, or experienced, or heard, not for people or events; I feel as though I've experienced nothing, learned nothing, I actually know less about most things than little schoolchildren do, and what I do know, I know so superficially that I am not even up to the task of the second question. I'm unable to think; my thinking keeps coming up against limits, I can grasp certain individual things in a flash, but coherent, sequential thinking is utterly impossible for me."

The image of the inexperienced ice skater was a natural one for him to choose; for both children and adults in Prague, skating was the main winter pastime, even during the war. Most ice-skating took place in rinks, where lessons were also offered and skates were rented. When the Vltava River froze over, safe areas were marked on the river, and skating beyond these markers was against the law. Even so, fatal accidents did occur repeatedly, especially among adolescents.

Not only is the "he" in Kafka's aphorism in danger of lagging behind the facts, but he also stands to lose track of them forever in the event of an accident. This is yet another expression of Kafka's fear that the increasing tension between his inner and outer worlds could eventually cause them to split apart for good (see the commentary on Aphorism 77).

68

Was ist fröhlicher als der Glaube an einen Hausgott!

What is more joyous than the belief in a household god!

Recorded on December 19 or 20, 1917. In the octavo notebook, the entry first read: "What is more joyous than the belief in a household god?—There is a down-and-outness beneath true knowledge and a childlike happy rising up!" Kafka was evidently hesitant about the second sentence: Initially he crossed it out, then he undid the deletion with a set of dots in the margin, yet when he copied the text onto the sheet he left it out all over again.

The revision process provides fresh evidence of Kafka's endeavor to make his writing as compact as possible. Although the second sentence contains an elucidation that helps the reader understand the conceptual thrust of the aphorism, it evidently struck Kafka as redundant.

A few years later Kafka adopted a very different tone in speaking about household gods: "To every invalid his household god, to the tubercular patient the god of suffocation. How can one bear his approach if one has no share in him even before the terrible union." Here again Kafka's naturopathic outlook shines through. People fall ill only when they have prepared the ground for that illness in advance, psychologically as well as physically. He also interpreted his own tuberculosis in this vein, especially in his letters from Zürau.

69

Theoretisch gibt es eine vollkommene Glücksmöglichkeit: An das Unzerstörbare in sich glauben und nicht zu ihm streben.

 Theoretically there is the possibility of attaining perfect happiness: by believing in the indestructible element in oneself and not striving toward it.

Recorded on December 19 or 20, 1917. Kafka revised the final words in the octavo notebook to "and no longer striving toward it" but did not carry over the revision onto the sheet.

An additional note in the octavo notebook (which he later crossed out) reads: "Believing means: liberating the indestructible element in oneself, or, more accurately: being indestructible, or, more accurately: being." This aphorism appears to conflict with that statement, although only if we assume that self-liberation—in the sense of unleashing one's own core— makes people happy. And this is not the case, as Kafka learned in his own life; on the contrary, it entails painful battles. (See also the commentary on Aphorism 70/71.)

The first condition specified in this aphorism, "believing in the indestructible element in oneself," is *always* fulfilled, according to Aphorism 50, albeit not always consciously. The second condition, by contrast, signifies a voluntary disavowal of self-liberation, which is why the happiness postulated by Kafka is also purely a "theoretical" one.

In a critique of Max Brod's *Paganism, Christianity, Judaism*, which Kafka wrote in a letter to Brod, he cited Aphorism 69, now substituting "the divine" for "the indestructible": "Perhaps the closest way to get to your view is to say: There is, theoretically, the possibility of attaining perfect happiness on earth, namely by believing in the determining divine principle and not striving toward it." This statement was adapted to the epistolary context (otherwise Kafka would have had to explain the term "indestructible"), but the idea of treating these terms as equivalent had aligned with his view for quite some time. Back in 1913 he had written to Felice Bauer: "But the things about you that have changed, Felice, were only minor details at the margins of your existence, which has unfolded before my eyes over the course of months, unfolded from an immutable divine core."

Das Unzerstörbare ist eines; jeder einzelne Mensch ist es und gleichzeitig ist es allen gemeinsam, daher die beispiellos untrennbare Verbindung der Menschen.

The indestructible is one thing; it is each individual person and at the same time it is something common to all, hence the supremely indivisible connection among people.

Recorded in Prague on December 24, 1917. Kafka added the number 71 subsequently, having evidently skipped over it in numbering the sheets.

While Aphorisms 50 and 69 speak of the "trust" and "belief" we bring (or ought to bring) to an indestructible core within us, this aphorism is the first instance of "the indestructible" being presupposed and stated as a fact.

The double perspective is already evident, however, in a note written one week before Aphorism 50: "Believing means: liberating the indestructible element in oneself, or, more accurately: being indestructible, or, more accurately: being." Although Kafka is attempting to pinpoint the concept of belief here, this formulation makes the indestructible not a mere matter of belief but a reality.

Another new element in Aphorism 70/71 is the social dimension of the indestructible. Since, as we are told in Aphorism 50, the indestructible can remain "forever hidden"—that is, unconscious—this must also apply to the community-building function of the indestructible. Kafka does not state this simple idea, but in 1917, in the midst of a world war, it easily sprang to mind.

72

Es gibt im gleichen Menschen Erkenntnisse, die bei völliger Verschiedenheit doch das gleiche Objekt haben, so dass wieder nur auf verschiedene Subjekte im gleichen Menschen rückgeschlossen werden muss.

In one and the same person there are insights that, for all their diversity, have one and the same object, and so one must infer that there are diverse subjects in one and the same person.

Recorded in Prague on December 24, 1917. In the octavo notebook, the verb "must" is instead "can," but the sheet has "must." Kafka crossed out the copy on the sheet.

In this aphorism Kafka acknowledges the existence of clashing subsystems within the human psyche, a concept he was presumably familiar with from the field of psychoanalysis, as we see by his use of the technical term "subject," which is unusual for Kafka and does not appear elsewhere in the octavo notebooks.

As we see in Aphorism 81, which was written three weeks later (see the commentary for that aphorism), Kafka continued to ponder this problem and came up with ideas that could scarcely be reconciled with Freud's metapsychology.

73

Er frisst den Abfall vom eigenen Tisch; dadurch wird er zwar ein Weilchen lang satter als alle, verlernt aber oben vom Tisch zu essen; dadurch hört dann aber auch der Abfall auf.

He devours the scraps falling from his own table; although this will make him more well-fed than the others for a little while, he forgets how to eat up at the table; yet that makes the scraps stop falling, too.

Recorded in Prague on December 27, 28, or 29, 1917.

In the context of the Zürau notes, this aphorism is thematically isolated. The metaphor chosen by Kafka accurately describes a favored but ominous strategy of authors whose powers of imagination are waning: they begin to "salvage" things they would have cast aside in better days. It is therefore reasonable to infer that here, as so often, Kafka is giving voice to his dissatisfaction with his own literary and intellectual productivity.

This metaphor suggests that either the *I* moves back and forth in an interior psychological space as though in a physical room, or that it is even fragmented, meaning that there are several subsystems whose courses of action diverge sharply (the one that "devours" up at the table and the one that does so down below). As Aphorisms 72 and 81 in particular show, Kafka was familiar with the notion of "diverse subjects in one and the same person."

74

Wenn das, was im Paradies zerstört worden sein soll, zerstörbar war, dann war es nicht entscheidend; war es aber unzerstörbar, dann leben wir in einem falschen Glauben.

If what is said to have been destroyed in Paradise was destructible, then it was not decisive; but if it was indestructible, then we are living in a false belief.

"[W]hat is said to have been destroyed in Paradise" can be understood—in the context of the Old Testament myth, which is referred to as the implicit source—in two ways. On the one hand, there is the provision of Paradise to serve man as a place to live. According to Aphorism 84, there is no indication, at least within the myth, that this provision has been rescinded. Paradise continues to exist. A note in the octavo notebooks states, "We were expelled from Paradise, but it was not destroyed." On the other hand, there is man's provision to live in Paradise. The provision was apparently changed, and we had to leave Paradise, yet in Kafka's view this expulsion is not a temporal occurrence but rather a perpetual, incompletable one beyond the grasp of our concept of time (see Aphorism 64). Consequently, then, our connection to Paradise is in no way "destroyed," and so in a sense our original provision continues on.

Kafka's "If . . . then" thus proves to be a rhetorical game. In his view, *no* actual destruction ensued in Paradise, not even in the act of expulsion; the human core remained intact, because it is indestructible (see Aphorisms 50 and 70/71). Here Kafka was leaving the interpretive horizon of the Mosaic religions, as he was well aware: "we are living in a false belief."

Aphorism 3 also hints at the possibility of a return to Paradise; for more on the motif of expulsion, see the commentary for Aphorism 3.

75

Prüfe Dich an der Menschheit. Den Zweifelnden macht sie zweifeln, den Glaubenden glauben.

Test yourself against mankind. It makes the doubter doubt, the believer believe.

Recorded between January 2 and 11, 1918. Kafka crossed it out after copying it onto the sheet.

The meaning of this directive is revealed in Aphorisms 50 and 70/71. My trust in something "indestructible" within me, that is, in my belonging to a (provisionally inaccessible) world of the spirit, is reinforced by mankind, because this indestructible element is "common to all" and can be recognized in others. So if I consciously experience this confirmation and reinforcement by way of other people, it indicates that my trust in my own indestructible core is something I'm already largely aware of and is a part of my identity.

Looking upon mankind *without* this belief, on the other hand, is more likely to engender doubts about the indestructible element and hence reinforce disbelief, since life within society and human history seems wholly dominated by the laws governing the world of the senses. But according to Aphorism 57, all that matters in the world of the senses is possessions, and Aphorism 54 even deems that world "Evil."

76

Dieses Gefühl: "hier ankere ich nicht" und gleich die wogende tragende Flut um sich fühlen!

———

Ein Umschwung. Lauernd, ängstlich, hoffend umschleicht die Antwort die Frage, sucht verzweifelt in ihrem unzugänglichen Gesicht, folgt ihr auf den sinnlosesten, d. h. von der Antwort möglichst wegstrebenden Wegen.

This feeling: "I am not dropping anchor here," and in no time feeling the swelling, buoyant tide all around!

———

A swerve. Lurking, skittish, hopeful, the answer prowls around the question, peers desperately into its unapproachable face, follows it on the most senseless paths, that is, those that veer as far away as possible from the answer.

The first text was recorded on January 12, 1918. Kafka copied the second text from a set of later manuscript pages and added to it on the sheet. This second text was written in late August 1920.

"I am not dropping anchor here" can be read as the visual expression of his insight that the empirical world of the senses cannot be "my" final destiny (a central theme of the Zürau notes; see the commentary on Aphorism 25). The new burst of energy that this insight (or, rather, this awareness) makes instantly palpable is not menacing, let alone devastating, but instead bears a person along, which, in the context of the aphorisms, is a fairly optimistic statement. Aphorism 78, written on the same day, is also about letting go.

The biographical context was presumably a contributing factor. A mere two weeks before writing the aphorism, Kafka had separated from Felice Bauer for good, after five years of excruciating attempts to "anchor" himself in a socially fulfilling life with her help. Even though their parting days in Prague were overshadowed by sorrow, Kafka also felt liberated. He wrote to Brod with uncharacteristic resolve: "What I have to do, I can do only alone. Become clear about the ultimate things." In this respect it may be no coincidence that he followed up this aphorism with a later supplement beginning with the words "A swerve."

This second text, while more impenetrable than Aphorism 76, also deals with a shift to a new level of insight. As the distance between question and answer continues to grow, the answer can no longer claim to be the answer to *this* question and needs to be formulated anew in order to remain meaningful. Accordingly, refuting an answer is not the only way to negate it; it can simply prove irrelevant if it has too little to do with the question.

77

Verkehr mit Menschen verführt zur Selbstbeobachtung.

Dealing with people engenders self-scrutiny.

Recorded on January 12, 1918.

Kafka considered intensive, occasionally even obsessive self-scrutiny one of his most serious psychological problems, because it alienated him from both the world and himself and had a deleterious effect on his self-esteem. He noted in his diary back in 1913: "Hatred of active self-scrutiny. Clarifications of one's soul, such as: Yesterday I was like this, and for this reason; today I'm like that, and for that reason.... To endure oneself calmly, without being hasty, to live as one must, not to run in circles like a dog." In the Zürau octavo notebooks he even characterized self-scrutiny as an instrument of Evil: "'Know thyself' does not mean 'Scrutinize thyself.' 'Scrutinize thyself' is what the serpent says."

The conflict persisted, however, and in the winter of 1921–1922 it evidently became especially pressing. "Inescapable commitment to self-scrutiny," Kafka noted in November. "If I am scrutinized by someone else, I must, of course, scrutinize myself as well; if I am scrutinized by no one else, I must scrutinize myself all the more precisely."

Two months later he wrote: "The clocks are not synchronized; the internal one races at a devilish or demoniac or in any case inhuman pace, the external one limps along at its usual speed. What else can happen but that the two different worlds split apart, and they do split apart, or at least tear away at each other in a fearful manner. There may be various reasons for the wild pace of the internal process: the most obvious one is self-scrutiny, which does not allow any idea to rest but chases up each one, only to become a notion of an idea that in turn is the object of renewed self-scrutiny."

In March 1922, Kafka mused, "What would it be like to choke to death on oneself? If urgent self-scrutiny were to make the opening through which one pours out into the world too small or even closed off altogether? At times I am not far from that."

78

Der Geist wird erst frei, wenn er aufhört, Halt zu sein.

The spirit becomes free only when it ceases to be a source of support.

Recorded on January 12, 1918. At some point after copying it onto the sheet, Kafka evidently came upon the idea of illustrating the message of this aphorism with an example. "If Noah were instead," he added in pencil, but blacked out these words with thick hatching.

The "world of the spirit" is a dominant theme in Kafka's octavo notebooks (see especially Aphorisms 54 and 62). "Spirit" as an individual capability, however, appears only once more, in a note composed in late February or early March 1918, presumably in reference to Kierkegaard, and there has more of a negative connotation: "The various forms of hopelessness at the various stations on the path." "He has too much spirit; he travels across the earth on his spirit as though he's on a magic chariot, even where there are no paths. And he cannot figure out on his own that there are no paths there. In this way his humble plea for others to follow him turns into tyranny, and his sincere belief that he is 'on the path' turns into haughtiness."

The connection between the aphorism and the later note is that in both cases, spirit is instrumentalized: as a source of support, as a vehicle, as a medium of intellectual vanity. The phrase "And he cannot figure out on his own" indicates that this form of brilliance can even lead to blind spots, to a lack of self-reflection.

79

Die sinnliche Liebe täuscht über die himmlische hinweg; allein könnte sie es nicht, aber da sie das Element der himmlischen Liebe unbewusst in sich hat, kann sie es.

Sensual love misleads us about heavenly love; it could not do so alone, but because it unknowingly has within it the element of heavenly love, it can.

Recorded on January 13, 1918.

Kafka draws both an ethical and an ontological distinction between the ("heavenly") world of the spirit and the world of the senses, such as in Aphorism 54: "what we call the world of the senses is the Evil in the spiritual realm." He concludes that sensual and sexual desire can also be ascribed to Evil (see Aphorisms 7 and 105). But because the world of the senses and the world of the spirit do not make up a coequal contrastive pair—the world of the senses being a mere shadow of the world of the spirit—even a purely earthly love has to contain a reflection of heavenly love, whether consciously or unconsciously. Kafka is drawing on a central concept of Plato's theory of forms: *méthexis* ("group sharing"), the ever-present sharing of every particular object or phenomenon of this world in its ideal archetype.

This idea makes logical sense, but it also illustrates the extent to which Kafka was subject to the influence of psychological conflicts in even the most abstract ramifications of his thinking. His letters and diaries show that the tension between love as a physical and an emotional experience tormented him increasingly as the years went on, until he was no longer capable of directing both forms of desire at one and the same woman. He considered this awareness so vital, even essential, that he even tried to dim Max Brod's hopes for erotic happiness: "'Tranquility, utter peace in eros' is something so colossal that it seems disproved by the very fact that you don't accept it unhesitatingly. Doubts could arise only if you would only call it by a less lofty name."

Kafka opened up to Milena Jesenská about his fears more than to anyone else. After once again recalling the affectionate time he had spent with her, he went on to write: "that is why you're right in saying that we were already one and I'm not the least bit afraid of this; quite the contrary, it is my only happiness and my only pride. . . . But it's simply that between this daytime world and the 'half hour in bed' you once scornfully wrote about, as though it were a matter for men, there is, as I see it, an abyss I cannot get over, most likely because I don't want to. Over there lies an affair of the night, absolutely and in every sense an affair of the night. . . ."

80

Wahrheit ist unteilbar, kann sich also selbst nicht erkennen; wer sie erkennen will, muss Lüge sein.

Truth is indivisible, and so it cannot recognize itself; anyone claiming to recognize it must be a lie.

Recorded on January 14, 1918. Kafka crossed it out after copying it onto the sheet.

Structurally, Kafka was taking up an argument he had applied to "Good" back in November. Two more entries in the octavo notebook read: "Evil knows of Good, but Good does not know of Evil." "Only Evil has self-knowledge." The indivisibility of the truth could be taken to mean that nothing is true that is not *utterly* true, and that anything that is almost true is inescapably untrue (a point of view that has found expression in the term "half-truth"). It is striking, however, that Kafka chose "lie" as an antonym for truth, as opposed to a falsehood or untruth. A lie is an *intentional* negation of the truth; its assessment is a matter not of epistemology but of ethics.

This aphorism is accordingly an example of how, for Kafka, ethical (*good/evil*) and epistemological categories (*true/untrue*) overlap. His emphatic concept of truth comprises not only what is right or coherent but, essentially, also what is good. (Closely related is also the conceptual pair *spiritual/sensory*; see the commentary on Aphorism 54.)

Consequently, then, Kafka is using the notion of the lie in an equally emphatic sense. *Being* a lie is far more than merely *uttering* a lie; it means *fundamentally* lying, that is, being evil.

The radical idea in this aphorism also had an impact on Kafka's self-perception as a writer. Since it is the task of literature to capture, if not the truth itself, at least its "light" (see Aphorism 63), the writer cannot himself be, or represent, truth—quite the contrary. Kafka appreciatively quoted Mörike's oral statement about Heinrich Heine: "He is a poet through and through, but I could not have spent fifteen minutes with him because of the lie at the core of his entire being." Kafka added this comment: "a brilliant and still-mysterious summary of what I think of the writer."

81

Niemand kann verlangen, was ihm im letzten Grunde schadet. Hat es beim einzelnen Menschen doch diesen Anschein—und den hat es vielleicht immer—so erklärt sich dies dadurch, dass jemand im Menschen etwas verlangt, was diesem jemand zwar nützt, aber einem zweiten jemand, der halb zur Beurteilung des Falles herangezogen wird, schwer schadet. Hätte sich der Mensch gleich anfangs, nicht erst bei der Beurteilung auf Seite des zweiten jemand gestellt, wäre der erste jemand erloschen und mit ihm das Verlangen.

No one can desire what ultimately harms him. Even if it has that appearance in a certain individual—and perhaps it always does—the explanation is that someone within the individual desires something that is of use to that someone but inflicts grievous harm on a second someone, who is brought in partly to judge the case. If the individual had sided with the second someone from the outset rather than waiting until the judgment, the first someone would have been defunct, and with him the desire.

Probably recorded on January 15, 1918.

The wording of the first clause—"No one can desire"—is easily misunderstood. The verb *verlangen* (desire) is not used in the more common sense of "demand," but rather in the nominal sense of *Verlangen haben nach etwas* (have a desire for something), as becomes evident when the word reappears as a noun at the close of the aphorism.

In Aphorism 72, Kafka had asserted the existence of several subjects within one and the same person, and he does so here as well, although this time not only on the cognitive level but in a more comprehensive sense that also encompasses desire.

As Kafka read through the psychological literature, he came to recognize quite clearly that the human psyche consists of subsystems that are related in complex ways and could work against as well as with one another. But this aphorism shows that Kafka pictured the interplay as far more transient than Freud did, contending that subpersonalities of this sort ("someones") could be made to disappear by a mere resolution on the part of the "individual" (that is, of the totality of a person). The divide is thus neither total nor irreversible.

There is no detailed documentation of Kafka's response to psychoanalysis, so the extent to which he was deliberately distancing himself from it in Aphorisms 72 and 81 cannot be determined with any certainty. In 1912 he wrote to the student Willy Haas, editor of the literary journal *Herderblätter*: "I do believe that one can read unprecedented things by Freud. Unfortunately I know little by him and a great deal by his disciples, and so I have only a great, yet empty respect for him."

For more on Kafka's critique of psychoanalysis, see the commentary on Aphorism 93.

82

Warum klagen wir wegen des Sündenfalls? Nicht seinetwegen sind wir aus dem Paradiese vertrieben worden, sondern wegen des Baumes des Lebens, damit wir nicht von ihm essen.

Why do we complain about the Fall? That isn't why we were expelled from Paradise, but on account of the Tree of Life, lest we eat of it.

Recorded on January 20, 1918.

In the Old Testament myth of the Fall and the expulsion from Paradise, there are two forbidden trees: the Tree of Knowledge and the Tree of Life. Once Adam and Eve had eaten from the Tree of Knowledge, God announced to them that their punishment would consist of expulsion from Paradise and a lifetime of toil. He subsequently explained the necessity for the expulsion as follows: "And the Lord God said, The man has now become like one of us, knowing good and evil. He must not be allowed to reach out his hand and take also from the tree of life and eat, and live forever. So the Lord God banished him from the Garden of Eden."

As was characteristic for Kafka (see, for example, his prose pieces "The Silence of the Sirens" and "Prometheus"), he gave this myth a modern psychological twist. He read and interpreted the ancient words as though they were the psychologically comprehensible utterances of a human subject attempting to rationalize his own conduct (in the octavo notebooks he even called one of God's prophecies "wrong"; see the commentary on Aphorism 3). In Kafka's view, the issue was not actually the "Fall" and the ensuing punishment at all but rather the move to deprive us permanently of access to the Tree of Life.

This shift in balance from the Old Testament source indicates a diminution of the significance of the Fall and a considerable enhancement of the role of the Tree of Life. Kafka drew the ethical conclusions of this reevaluation in the following Aphorism, 83, which may have been written on the same day.

For more on the expulsion from Paradise, see Aphorisms 3, 64, 74, and 84.

Wir sind nicht nur deshalb sündig, weil wir
vom Baum der Erkenntnis gegessen haben, sondern
auch deshalb, weil wir vom Baum des Lebens
noch nicht gegessen haben. Sündig ist der Stand,
in dem wir uns befinden, unabhängig von
Schuld.

nicht von ihm essen.

~~Sie und so ~~ ~~Gott bedarm~~ ~~getrennt~~
~~welchter~~ ~~Sohn und mit eine~~
~~Gott~~ ~~treue~~ verbunden: Der
Sündenfall trennt ihn von
ihm, der Baum, des Lebens
trennt ihn von uns

Wir sind nicht deshalb sündig
weil wir vom Baum der Erkenntnis
gegessen haben, sondern auch deshalb weil wir vom
Baum des Lebens noch nicht gegessen
haben

Sündig ist der Stand in dem
wir uns befinden, unabhängig
von Schuld

Baum des Lebens — Herr des Lebens

Wir wurden aus dem Paradies
vertrieben, aber zerstört wurde
es nicht. ✝

Wir wurden geschaffen um im
Paradies zu leben, das Paradies

83

Wir sind nicht nur deshalb sündig, weil wir vom Baum der Erkenntnis gegessen haben, sondern auch deshalb, weil wir vom Baum des Lebens noch nicht gegessen haben. Sündig ist der Stand, in dem wir uns befinden, unabhängig von Schuld.

We are sinful not only because we have eaten of the Tree of Knowledge but also because we have yet to eat of the Tree of Life. The state in which we find ourselves is sinful, irrespective of guilt.

Recorded on January 20 or 21, 1918. In the octavo notebook, there is a dividing line between the two sentences, which Kafka initially regarded as separate notations.

Kafka's original wording drew a sharper, more exclusionary distinction: "We are sinful not because we have eaten of the Tree of Knowledge but because we did not eat of the Tree of Life."

This aphorism continues and radicalizes the reflection in Aphorism 82; now it stands in opposition to religious tradition by maintaining that adherence to a divine command—not to eat from the Tree of Life—is sinful.

A later statement in the octavo notebooks shows how Kafka arrived at this reassessment: "For us there are two kinds of truth, as it is represented by the Tree of Knowledge and the Tree of Life: the truth of the active principle and the truth of the static principle; in the first, Good separates itself from Evil, and the second is nothing but Good itself, knowing neither of Good nor of Evil. The first truth is really and truly given to us, the second just subliminally. That is the sorrowful spectacle. The cheerful aspect is that the first truth belongs merely to the moment, the second to eternity, which is why the first truth also fades out in the light of the second."

Kafka thus construed eating from the Tree of Life as a transition into a life of a higher order, one that no longer relies on a distinction between Good and Evil, because it is itself Good. (Similar to the conceptual framework in Aphorism 37, which subordinates mere *possessing* to *being*.) The Fall, which is depicted in great detail in the Old Testament, loses in significance and "fades out." Of course this notion rests on the hope that access to the "true" life does not remain barred to us in perpetuity. As Kafka sees it, hope is justified because the expulsion from Paradise (for more on this motif, see Aphorisms 3, 74, and 84) is not bound to a specific time and so not subject to being finalized (see Aphorism 64).

84

Wir wurden geschaffen, um im Paradies zu leben, das Paradies war bestimmt uns zu dienen. Unsere Bestimmung ist geändert worden; dass dies auch mit der Bestimmung des Paradieses geschehen wäre, wird nicht gesagt.

We were created to live in Paradise, and Paradise was destined to serve us. Our destiny has been altered; it is not stated that this has also happened to the destiny of Paradise.

Recorded on January 20 or 21, 1918. In the octavo notebook, the second sentence is formulated apodictically: "Our destiny has been altered, but not the destiny of Paradise." It was only when Kafka copied the text onto the sheet that he qualified this statement with reference to the Old Testament myth as a source ("it is not stated"), as he had in Aphorism 74.

In the octavo notebook, Kafka had a choice between four successive notes with the same subject matter to use for his collection of aphorisms. The other three, which he later crossed out, read: "We were expelled from Paradise, but it was not destroyed." "Almost right to the end of the account of the Fall, it remains possible that the Garden of Eden is cursed together with man. Only man was cursed, not the Garden of Eden." "The expulsion from Paradise was in a sense a bit of good fortune, for if we had not been expelled, Paradise would have had to be destroyed." Kafka opted for the note that sounded most concise and even has a juridical undertone.

The continued existence of Paradise—even though it remains beyond the grasp of our temporal powers of imagination—is of great significance for Kafka's concept of the "indestructible"; see Aphorism 74 and the accompanying commentary.

On the motif of the expulsion, see also the commentary on Aphorism 3.

85

Das Böse ist eine Ausstrahlung des menschlichen Bewusstseins in bestimmten Übergangsstellungen. Nicht eigentlich die sinnliche Welt ist Schein, sondern ihr Böses, das allerdings für unsere Augen die sinnliche Welt bildet.

Evil is an emanation of human consciousness at certain transitional points. It is not actually the world of the senses that is illusory but the Evil within it, which, however, in our eyes is what makes up the world of the senses.

Recorded on January 20 or 21, 1918.In the octavo notebook, this entry initially ended with the words: "but the Evil within it, which, however, in our eyes is the same thing." Kafka made the revision before copying the text onto the sheet.

It seems difficult to reconcile this aphorism with the messages in several others, which characterize Evil as a force that acts upon man from the outside. Here, Evil is attributable solely to man, while Aphorism 54 tells us: "what we call the world of the senses is the Evil in the spiritual realm."

Still, that earlier aphorism clarifies what Kafka means by a "transitional point," as he goes on to write: "and what we call Evil is only a momentary necessity in our eternal development." Evil is embedded in human development, while the term "necessity" signals that this is not only a psychological phenomenon but also a spiritual one, independent of our will. In Aphorism 105, consequently, not only man in the current state but rather "this world" as a whole is designated as a "transition," an interim stage on the way to a world of a higher order.

The seeming contradictions evidently result from Kafka's inclination to regard the phenomenon of Evil from ontological, ethical, and psychological perspectives, and he did not always clearly differentiate between these perspectives and levels of meaning.

On the subject of Evil, see also Aphorisms 19, 28, 29, 39, 51, 54, 55, 86, 95, 100, 105, and the commentary on Aphorism 7. On the connections between the world of the senses and the world of the spirit, see also Aphorisms 57, 62, and 97.

86

Seit dem Sündenfall sind wir in der Fähigkeit zur Erkenntnis des Guten und Bösen im Wesentlichen gleich; trotzdem suchen wir gerade hier unsere besonderen Vorzüge. Aber erst jenseits dieser Erkenntnis beginnen die wahren Verschiedenheiten. Der gegenteilige Schein wird durch Folgendes hervorgerufen: Niemand kann sich mit der Erkenntnis allein begnügen, sondern muss sich bestreben, ihr gemäss zu handeln. Dazu aber ist ihm die Kraft nicht mitgegeben, er muss daher sich zerstören, selbst auf die Gefahr hin, sogar dadurch die notwendige Kraft nicht zu erhalten, aber es bleibt ihm nichts anderes übrig, als dieser letzte Versuch. (Das ist auch der Sinn der Todesdrohung beim Verbot des Essens vom Baume der Erkenntnis; vielleicht ist das auch der ursprüngliche Sinn des natürlichen Todes.) Vor diesem Versuch nun fürchtet er sich; lieber will er die Erkenntnis des Guten und Bösen rückgängig machen; (Die Bezeichnung "Sündenfall" geht auf diese Angst zurück) aber das Geschehene kann nicht rückgängig sondern nur getrübt werden. Zu diesem Zweck entstehen die Motivationen. Die ganze Welt ist ihrer voll, ja die ganze sichtbare Welt ist vielleicht nichts anderes, als eine Motivation des einen Augenblick lang ruhenwollenden Menschen. Ein Versuch, die Tatsache der Erkenntnis zu fälschen, die Erkenntnis erst zum Ziel zu machen.

Since the Fall we have been essentially alike in our ability to know Good and Evil; even so, this is precisely where we seek our special advantages. It is only when we get beyond this knowledge, however, that the true differences begin. The opposite appearance is produced in the following way: no one can be content with the knowledge alone, but must endeavor to act in accordance with it. Yet he is not endowed with the strength for this, so he must destroy himself, even at the risk of not receiving the necessary strength, but he has no choice other than to make this final effort. (This is also the meaning of the threat of death accompanying the prohibition on eating of the Tree of Knowledge; perhaps this is also the original meaning of natural death.) He fears this effort; he would rather undo the knowledge of Good and Evil; (The term "the Fall" derives from this fear) but it cannot be undone, only blurred.[1] Motivations arise for this purpose. The entire world is full of them, indeed, the entire visible world may be nothing other than a motivation of man's wish to rest for a moment. An effort to falsify the fact of knowledge, to turn the knowledge into the goal.

1 *Translator's note*: The unusual placement of the semicolon and the capitalized parenthetical remark in this aphorism (after "the knowledge of Good and Evil") adhere to Kafka's punctuation in the manuscript.

Recorded on January 22, 23, or 24, 1918. Because of the length of this note, Kafka also used the reverse side of sheet 86.

Kafka may have initially regarded the first two sentences of this aphorism as a self-contained text. In the octavo notebook, two more notations (including Aphorism 87) follow, and only then the continuation of Aphorism 86.

This continuation was originally even longer, and ended with the sentence: "But under all the smoke there is the fire and he whose feet are burning will not be saved by the fact that he sees nothing but dark smoke everywhere." Kafka crossed out this sentence, however, before copying the text onto the sheet.

The core concept of this aphorism is psychological in nature. All of us basically know what is Good and what is Evil, but we don't have the strength to carry out something purely Good. We are eager to do so, yet we run the risk of overreaching ("destroying"), and we consequently shrink back from the attempt, opting instead to water down our knowledge of Good and Evil retroactively; that is, we invent reasons ("motivations") to pass off our own actions as good when they are objectively not good, and thus to calm ourselves down. It is only in this art of rationalization that people differ substantially.

The text seems especially complex because Kafka embedded this idea in metaphysical speculations, which, in turn, drew their images from the Old Testament myth. This speculative turn of thought reaches its pinnacle in the penultimate sentence, where psychology and metaphysics come together: Perhaps, Kafka mused, our world is merely an obstacle created by man, which allows us to cease "for a moment," with a clear conscience, our grueling battle to attain Good—and to act as though it has yet to be clarified what "Good" truly means.

For more on the relationship between Good and Evil, see Aphorisms 27, 51, 55, and 105, along with the commentary on Aphorism 7. For more on the Fall of Man at the Tree of Knowledge, see Aphorisms 82 and 83, and the commentaries on Aphorisms 3 and 11/12.

87

Ein Glaube wie ein Fallbeil, so schwer, so leicht.

A belief like a guillotine, as heavy, as light.

Recorded on January 22, 23, or 24, 1918. On the intertwining of Aphorisms 86 and 87 in the manuscript, see the commentary on Aphorism 86.

The octavo notebook indicates that Kafka first intended to write: "A belief, heavy as a guillotine . . ." As in numerous other revisions, he was seeking the pithiest linguistic formulation.

In this aphorism, Kafka is clearly addressing two different stages of reflection. Belief is "light" as long as it is accepted as something that is self-evident, or even spreads its effect unbeknownst to those receiving it—such as the belief in life, which is not a psychological realization but rather arises from life itself (see Aphorism 109).

But belief grows "heavy" as soon as it is permeated with thought. It is "heavy" because doubts arise, doubts that tend to intensify under the pressure of life experience (see, for instance, Aphorism 75). It is also "heavy" in the sense of "weighty": Once we realize how much is dependent on belief—which, for Kafka, assumes virtually ontological status (see the commentary on Aphorism 37)—the obligation arises to be *expected* to believe.

Eventually the gap between our ability to believe and our limited options to live in accordance with this belief grows conspicuous. Aphorism 69, for example, recommends as the path to happiness: "believing in the indestructible element in oneself and not striving toward it." Kafka conceded that this was no more than a theoretical possibility, since every belief, once entering our consciousness, pressures us to implement it.

Kafka's choice of the drastic image of the guillotine underscores even further the perils these aporias confront us with. "[N]o one can be content with the knowledge alone," Aphorism 86 tells us, "but must endeavor to act in accordance with it, yet he is not endowed with the strength for this, so he must destroy himself."

88

Der Tod ist vor uns, etwa wie im Schulzimmer an der Wand ein Bild der Alexanderschlacht. Es kommt darauf an, durch unsere Taten noch in diesem Leben das Bild zu verdunkeln oder gar auszulöschen.

Death is before us, rather like a picture of the Battle of Alexander on the classroom wall. It is imperative for us to use our actions to obscure or even obliterate this picture in our lifetimes.

Recorded on January 25, 26, or 27, 1918. Kafka did not add the phrase "in our lifetimes" until copying the text onto the sheet.

Even before that, he had tried to inject chronological specificity into this statement; in the octavo notebook, above the words "It is imperative" the word fragment *erwach* is inserted in ink, then crossed out. It is a trace of a revision, the intended result of which would presumably have read: "It is imperative for us, once we are grown up [*erwachsen*] . . . ," or, more concisely, "It is imperative for us, once grown up . . ."

A reproduction of the so-called Alexander Mosaic (2nd cent. BC, found in Pompei in 1831), comprising more than one million pieces of stone and glass, was on display at the Altstädter Gymnasium in Prague, the secondary school Kafka attended. The repeated references to Alexander indicate that the large-sized depiction of a battle, presumably the battle at Issus against the Persians, left a deep and lasting impression on the young Kafka (see the commentaries on Aphorisms 34 and 39).

Aphorism 88 is the only one that has death as its central theme, and portrays death as an ethical challenge. We have only indirect evidence of Kafka's philosophical attitude toward biological death, but he certainly did not regard it as an absolute boundary, because that would have been incompatible with his notion of an "indestructible" core of all that is human, and with the idea of an "eternal development" (see Aphorisms 50, 54, 69, and 70/71).

Kafka's emotional relationship to his own looming death changed in the Zürau months, in a manner that—as it seemed to his friends—was hardly conducive to a recovery. He wrote to Max Brod: "The only certainty is that there is nothing to which I would surrender with more complete confidence than to death." On the same day, he wrote in his diary: "I would therefore entrust myself to death. Remnant of a faith. Return to the father. Great Day of Atonement."

90

Zwei Möglichkeiten: sich unendlich klein machen oder es sein. Das erste ist Vollendung also Untätigkeit, das zweite Beginn, also Tat.

Two possibilities: to make oneself infinitely small, or to be so. The first is perfection, that is, inaction, the second is beginning, that is, action.

Recorded on January 28, 29, or 30, 1918. Kafka crossed it out after copying it onto the sheet.

Kafka changed the numbering of the sheet from 89 to 90. It is unclear whether there ever was a sheet numbered 89.

There is some indication that Kafka inadvertently transposed the terms belonging to "the first" and "the second" in this text. (The editions of the octavo notebooks that Max Brod oversaw rearranged the pairings without comment.) It would be hard to see how making onself infinitely small could be equated with inaction.

Kafka's distinctly defensive character helps us understand why he regarded smallness rather than largeness as an attribute of perfection. He had a propensity for reconciling humiliating social experiences with his sense of self-worth by taking personal charge of them, such as by responding to criticism from others by leveling even sharper criticism at himself.

The experience of smallness was in a similar vein. Kafka felt he was "made small" when overwhelmed in a social setting ("I felt so very small while they all stood around me like giants," Kafka wrote on the occasion of a visit to Felice Bauer's family, although he stood six feet tall), yet for this very reason he endeavored to make himself socially inconspicuous, that is, to offer the smallest possible target from the outset. Compare this remark to Milena Jesenská: "In the atmosphere of your life with him [her husband], I really am just the mouse in the 'big house,' allowed to run freely across the carpet once a year at the most."

Aphorism 94 illustrates Kafka's attempt to justify the strategy of self-reduction on an intellectual level as well.

91

Zur Vermeidung eines Wort-Irrtums: Was tätig zerstört werden soll, muss vorher ganz fest gehalten worden sein; was zerbröckelt, zerbröckelt, kann aber nicht zerstört werden.

To avoid a verbal slip-up: Anything that should be actively destroyed must first be held quite firmly; what crumbles, crumbles, but cannot be destroyed.

Recorded on January 28, 29, or 30, 1918. Kafka crossed it out after copying it onto the sheet.

The octavo notebook contains a rough linguistic version of this aphorism, which Kafka revised before copying the text onto sheet 91. The textual appearance indicates that this revision was made in one go; the rough version read as follows: "To avoid a slip-up: Anything that should be destroyed must first be held firmly; what crumbles cannot be destroyed."

Once again, Kafka was adhering to the logic of the image; the reader has to visualize the process in order to grasp the argument. Destruction and crumbling may lead to the same practical result, but the terms belong to very different ranges of associations: the one designates an active feat, the other a naturally occurring process. For this reason, Kafka used the phrase "verbal slip-up."

The difference becomes significant chiefly in the ethical context, as the words "actively" and "should" indicate. If I need to destroy something, I have to take it in hand, engage with it, grasp it in a visual sense; distancing myself is not enough. But if something is bound to fall apart right before my eyes anyway, it is no longer ethically relevant.

92

Die erste Götzenanbetung war gewiss Angst vor den Dingen, aber damit zusammenhängend Angst vor der Notwendigkeit der Dinge und damit zusammenhängend Angst vor der Verantwortung für die Dinge. So ungeheuer erschien diese Verantwortung dass man sie nicht einmal einem einzigen Aussermenschlichen aufzuerlegen wagte, denn auch durch Vermittlung bloss eines Wesens wäre die menschliche Verantwortung noch nicht genug erleichtert worden, der Verkehr mit nur einem Wesen wäre noch allzusehr von Verantwortung befleckt gewesen, deshalb gab man jedem Ding die Verantwortung für sich selbst, mehr noch, man gab diesen Dingen auch noch eine verhältnismässige Verantwortung für den Menschen.

The first idol worship was certainly a fear of things, but, in conjunction with that, fear of the necessity of things and, in conjunction with that, fear of responsibility for the things. That responsibility seemed so colossal that people didn't even dare to impose it on one single extra-human, for the mediation of one being would not suffice to alleviate human responsibility, and contact with only one being would have been too tainted by responsibility, so each thing was given the responsibility for itself, and what is more, these things were also given a measure of responsibility for humankind.

Recorded on January 28, 29, or 30, 1918. In the original version, this text contained an introductory sentence, which also served as the opening line for the second Zürau octavo notebook: "By imposing too great a responsibility, or, rather, all of it, upon yourself, you crush yourself"—and it ended with a summation, which is also missing from sheet 92: "People could not manage to do enough in creating counterweights; this naive world was the most complex one that had ever existed, and its naivete expressed itself exclusively as brutal consistency."

The revision makes it clear that although he was furnishing a speculative justification for animism, his main concern was once again ethical: the issue of responsibility. The long second sentence in particular suggests that people in prehistoric times had made a free choice between believing in one, in several, or in countless gods, and they decided according to the criterion of the greatest possible alleviation of responsibility, delegating as much of it as they could. According to the deleted final sentence this was anything but a naive decision, but it was possible—and here Kafka's critique becomes palpable—only with a willingness to accede to an extremely complex and thus grueling situation.

For a different function of deism, which also entailed alleviation, see Aphorism 50.

93

Zum letztenmal Psychologie!

Psychology, for the last time!

Recorded on February 1, 1918, and crossed out after being copied onto the sheet.

In the octavo notebook, Kafka noted in the preceding line: "Lenz letters," in reference to the newly published *Briefe von und an J.M.R. Lenz* [Letters from and to J.M.R. Lenz], which Kafka had received as a gift from his publisher, Kurt Wolff. The first paragraph of the editor's introduction states: "In order to justify an edition of a complete collection of letters . . . the person it highlights needs to offer so much psychological interest that it is worth getting to know the person from all angles." This statement may have prompted Kafka to write Aphorism 93.

Shortly thereafter, in a note dated February 25, Kafka explained why he had had quite enough of psychology: "Psychology is a reading of mirror writing, which is to say that it is laborious and, in regard to the invariably correct result, fruitful, but nothing has actually happened." But Kafka crossed out this note in a particularly striking manner, with a whole cluster of lines.

Four months earlier he had noted: "Psychology is the description of the reflection of earthly world in the heavenly plane, or, to put it more accurately, the description of a reflection such as we, steeped in our earthly nature, conceive of it, for no reflection actually occurs; we see only earth whichever way we turn."

Kafka read psychological treatises primarily during his university years; at the age of nineteen, he attended a lecture on "Basic Questions of Descriptive Psychology" by Anton Marty, a devoted follower of Franz Brentano. Brentano's psychological theory, which categorically excluded unconscious mental acts, was also discussed in the Louvre Circle, a philosophical group to which Kafka belonged for some time.

He later applied his general skepticism of psychology to his stance on psychoanalysis. In a letter to Max Brod, written in Zürau, Kafka characterized psychoanalytic literature as something "that is remarkably filling at first, but after just a short time one feels the same old hunger."

Nevertheless, traces of basic psychoanalytic premises are clearly recognizable in Kafka's Zürau writings; see, for example, Aphorisms 72 and 81 along with the accompanying commentaries.

94

Zwei Aufgaben des Lebensanfangs: Deinen Kreis immer mehr einschränken und immer wieder nachprüfen, ob Du Dich nicht irgendwo ausserhalb deines Kreises versteckt hältst.

Two tasks at the beginning of life: to keep reining in your sphere, and to keep checking whether you might have gone into hiding somewhere outside your sphere.

Recorded on February 1, 1918.

This aphorism reflects Kafka's view that all of us are endowed with a spiritual imprint, a "nature" we should adopt and continue to develop purposefully (a view that also harmonized with the pedagogical impulses of the back-to-nature movement, which Kafka affirmed). This approach requires first and foremost a focus on the essentials; anything beyond that can do no more than serve as a temporary "hiding place" from the demands of one's own nature.

Kafka went even further in another note he wrote in Zürau, defining the fulfillment of the task dictated by a person's own nature as the only possible justification for human life: "No one creates more here than his spiritual potential; it is of lesser importance that he seems to be working for his food, clothing, etc., for with every visible morsel handed to him he is given an invisible one as well, with every visible garment an invisible garment as well, and so forth. That is every human being's justification. It seems as though he is underpinning his existence with belated justifications, but that is only psychological mirror-writing; he is actually constructing his life on his justifications."

Early on, he was assailed by doubts as to whether he himself, for the sake of literature, might have reined in his own sphere too far: "A concentration on writing is quite easy to recognize in me. When it became clear in my organism that writing was the most productive direction for my being, everything pressed in that direction and left bare all abilities aimed at the joys of sex, eating, drinking, philosophical reflection, and music above all. I withered away in all those directions."

In Kafka's later years, tuberculosis and dwindling social contacts rendered him less and less able to derive benefit from notions of restrictiveness and the whole related range of ascetic associations. Kafka's "hunger artist" in the story of that name also follows his prescribed path, but he is not a positive character.

95

Das Böse ist manchmal in der Hand wie ein Werkzeug, erkannt oder uner-
kannt, lässt es sich, wenn man den Willen hat, ohne Widerspruch zur Seite
legen.

Evil is sometimes like a tool in the hand: recognized or unrecognized, it
can be laid aside without opposition if one has the will to do so.

Recorded on February 2, 1918; Kafka crossed it out after copying it onto the sheet.

In the octavo notebook, Evil can be laid aside "calmly." Evidently, though, Kafka was bothered by the semantic ambiguity—*who* is calm?—and he revised it to read "without opposition." The octavo notebook displays another attempt at a metaphorical formulation: "be laid aside, Evil in hibernation, a bewitched Evil, indeed it falls apart under your gaze."

In view of the large number of his notes that address the influence and ingenuity of Evil (see Aphorisms 7, 19, 28, 29, 39, 55, 105), the claim that all it takes to paralyze Evil is the "will" seems surprising at first.

But Kafka held that each individual contains an "indestructible" core connecting him to both the human community and a sphere that lies beyond the world of the senses (see Aphorisms 50 and 70/71). Consequently, we may *do* any amount of evil but not *be* quintessentially evil. The influence of Evil reaches its limit when man attains an awareness of his human core. As Aphorism 51 tells us, Evil can "not become man." And Aphorism 100 states that it is not even possible to "believe" in Evil.

Kafka's contemporaries reported that he adhered to this maxim in his social behavior as well. Max Brod noted in 1918: "The good way he has of seeing the positive side in everyone (even in adversaries), where they are right, where they have no other choice . . . has often given me comfort, provided me a firm basis. His confidence that a pure intention, that substantive work is never meaningless, that nothing will be for naught—I rely on that."

96

Die Freuden dieses Lebens sind nicht die <u>seinen</u>, sondern <u>unsere</u> Angst vor dem Aufsteigen in ein höheres Leben; die Qualen dieses Lebens sind nicht die seinen, sondern unsere Selbstqual wegen jener Angst.

The joys of this life are not <u>its</u> own, but rather <u>our</u> fear of rising up to a higher life; the torments of this life are not its own, but rather our self-torment on account of that fear.

Recorded on February 3, 1918. The two underlinings were already in the octavo notebook. Instead of "our fear" he originally wrote "our hesitation."

The revision makes it clear how semantically condensed this aphorism is. Kafka forces readers to flesh out, on their own, thought processes that have been compressed into a single word, much like reading a sentence that consists only of commonly used abbreviations. The joys "are" thus not fear in the literal sense, but rather the expression of our reluctance to let go of "this life"; reluctance, in turn, is an expression of our fear.

Accordingly, joys exist only because we try to avoid looking toward a "higher" world. Torments, by contrast, exist because we are secretly aware that this is merely a diversionary tactic.

This idea is anti-psychological in nature, and is more easily understood in combination with Aphorisms 97, 102, and 103, which explicitly address the subject of "suffering" (in Aphorism 96 Kafka evidently used the synonym "torments" instead in order to pave the way to the term "self-torment"). In those aphorisms it becomes more apparent that he has in mind a collective behavior that arises from human "nature," not an individual failure that could be avoided with isolated ascetic and moral efforts. The same applies to the misconception that joys and suffering are absolute opposites (see especially the following aphorism, 97, written one day later).

Kafka's notion of a "higher life" is based on the distinction he draws between the world of the senses and the world of the spirit (see, for example, Aphorisms 54, 57, 62, 85, 97), and also on his assumption that mankind undergoes an eternal development, which can be interpreted as gradual "rising up" (see Aphorisms 6 and 54, and the commentary on Aphorism 38).

Nur hier ist Leiden Leiden. Nicht so, als
ob die, welche hier leiden, anderswo wegen
dieses Leidens erhöht werden sollen, sondern
so daß das was in dieser Welt Leiden
heißt, in einer andern Welt, unverändert
und nur befreit von seinem Gegensatz,
Seligkeit ist.

die einzige Verbindung zwischen dieser
Welt und dem Künstlichen [hier
ist Leiden —
Leiden. Nicht als ob die welche
hier leiden anderswo wegen dieses
Leidens erhöht werden sollen,
sondern wo das dieses Leiden
das ... in dieser Welt
Leiden ... in einer andern
Welt, unverändert und nur
befreit von ihrer Gegensätz-
lichkeit ist.]

Motiven dieser Welt, wäre nur dann
die tiefeste, wenn wir sie als stets
behaftende, nie unserer Einsicht oder
Entnehmung entgebend hätten, so
wie ersten Ihre Weise d.h. wider-
sprechend unserem Sinn und letzten
wenn wir imstande wären wie

97

Nur hier ist Leiden Leiden. Nicht so, als ob die, welche hier leiden, anderswo wegen dieses Leidens erhöht werden sollen, sondern so, dass das was in dieser Welt Leiden heisst, in einer andern Welt, unverändert und nur befreit von seinem Gegensatz, Seligkeit ist.

Only here is suffering suffering. Not in the way that those who suffer here are to be elevated in some other place on account of this suffering, but in such a way that what in this world is called suffering is in another world, unchanged and only freed from its opposite, bliss.

Recorded on February 4, 1918. In the octavo notebook, the text has an introductory sentence: "Suffering is the positive element in this world, indeed it is the only link between this world and the positive."

The reason that the first sentence is missing in the copy might be that the "positive" brings into play an additional concept that is not readily compatible with the "other world." See Aphorism 54, which speaks of "Evil" in the world of the spirit, and the commentary for Aphorism 27.

In Aphorisms 96, 102, and 103, Kafka also interpreted human suffering in a manner that amounted to a substantial reassessment of this term. Aphorism 97 makes clear that this reassessment needs to go much further than it has in the monotheistic religions, which only ease and downplay the significance of suffering by holding out the prospect of rewards.

Instead, Kafka adhered to a conceptual model that was prefigured in Hegel's tripartite dialectical sublation and was also found in Kierkegaard. In this aphorism, suffering is *aufgehoben* in the threefold sense of the German verb: it is destroyed (suffering will no longer be suffering), it is preserved (because it remains "unchanged"), and it is elevated ("liberated" from its opposite, it becomes "bliss"; see also the commentary on Aphorism 103).

It is unclear whether this intellectual appropriation—which is striking in view of Kafka's normally image-based thinking—can be attributed to his rereading of Kierkegaard in February 1918. In late March, in a letter to Max Brod, Kafka listed some of Kierkegaard's terminology that especially impressed him, including, once again, "the concept of the 'dialectical.'"

For more on the distinction between "this world" and "another world"—which Kafka generally defines as the distinction between the world of the senses and the world of the spirit—see Aphorisms 54, 57, 62, 85, and 96.

98

Die Vorstellung von der unendlichen Weite und Fülle des Kosmos ist das Ergebnis der zum Äussersten getriebenen Mischung von mühevoller Schöpfung und freier Selbstbesinnung.

The notion of the infinite expanse and plenitude of the cosmos is the result of the combination, taken to the extreme, of arduous creation and free self-contemplation.

Recorded on February 6, 1918. Kafka crossed it out on the sheet after copying it.

Because this aphorism has no thematic equivalent in the entire set, and the octavo notebooks contain no preliminary wordings or substantial revisions, it is one of the most difficult to decipher.

Here Kafka was attempting to establish that our concept of the cosmos is essentially a projection, by drawing a distinction between two states of human aggregation. One is "free self-contemplation," which, as a purely psychological movement, does not come up against any external obstacles, experiences neither temporal nor spatial restrictions, and has an inexhaustible reservoir at its disposal. Another is "creation" as a practical activity, which is always "arduous" because it has to grapple with the resistance of the material, the laws of logic and causality, and limited energy reserves.

In real life, the two states overlap, since any practical endeavor is accompanied by mental activity but also wears out this activity and in the process restricts it. If it were actually possible to combine the two states— "to the extreme," as Kafka says—creation would occur with virtually the same freedom as thinking. The result would be a creative explosion of both infinite magnitude and infinite abundance—and the cosmos appears to us as its image.

The impetus for these reflections may have been the rules governing literary production, which Kafka also touched upon in his diary. The imagination, running free, pushes ahead to create a literary cosmos, while the material—language and the requirements of literary form and communicability in particular—sets limits on the creative act and invariably provides only a glimpse of the infinite potential hidden behind it.

99

Wieviel bedrückender als die unerbittlichste Überzeugung von unserem ge-
genwärtigen sündhaften Stand ist selbst die schwächste Überzeugung von
der einstigen ewigen Rechtfertigung unserer Zeitlichkeit. Nur die Kraft im
Ertragen dieser zweiten Überzeugung, welche in ihrer Reinheit die erste voll
umfasst, ist das Mass des Glaubens.

———

Manche nehmen an, dass neben dem grossen Urbetrug noch in jedem Fall
eigens für sie ein kleiner besonderer Betrug veranstaltet wird, dass also wenn
ein Liebesspiel auf der Bühne aufgeführt wird, die Schauspielerin ausser
dem verlogenen Lächeln für ihren Geliebten auch noch ein besonders hinter-
hältiges Lächeln für den ganz bestimmten Zuschauer auf der letzten Galerie
hat. Das heisst zu weit gehen.

How much more oppressive than the most uncompromising conviction
of our current state of sin is even the weakest conviction of the erstwhile
eternal justification for our temporality. Only the fortitude to endure this
second conviction, which, in its purity, entirely encompasses the first, is
the measure of faith.

———

There are some who assume that besides the great primal deception there
is also, in every case, a special little deception arranged expressly for them,
so that if a romantic comedy is performed on the stage, the actress, in
addition to the duplicitous smile for her lover, has another particularly
conniving smile for that very specific spectator in the top balcony. That
is going too far.

The first text was recorded on February 9, 1918. Kafka copied the second text out of a set of later notes and added to it on the sheet. This second text was written in late August 1920.

Two thematically related reflections immediately precede his writing the first text in the octavo notebook: "But eternity is not temporality at a standstill [horizontal line] The oppressive aspect of the concept of the eternal is the incomprehensible justification, incomprehensible to us, that time must experience in eternity and the consequent justification of ourselves as we are."

What makes the idea of the "justification, incomprehensible to us" so "oppressive," and why it demands so much "belief," becomes evident once we bear in mind Kafka's concept of time. "This world cannot be followed by a world beyond," we read in the octavo notebook, "for the world beyond is eternal, hence it cannot have a temporal connection to this world." In other words, only from our limited view is there an "erstwhile" justification; in actuality our finite time is surrounded by eternity, and thus justification is required at every single moment. Aphorism 40 provides an even more trenchant formulation, invoking the term "court martial."

The beginning of the second text initially read: "Mistrustful people have always struck me as ridiculous, because they are people who assume that . . ." Kafka first changed that wording to "People who are always mistrustful are those who assume that . . ." In copying the text onto the sheet, he reduced the phrase to "There are some who assume that . . ."

The last sentence initially read: "Foolish arrogance." Here, too, the revision was made as he was copying the text. Both revisions take back and neutralize the negative assessments of human behavior.

Kafka's use of the phrase "great primal deception" refers to our illusion that the earthly world of the senses is real and substantial, although there is actually nothing but a world of the spirit (see Aphorism 62).

100

Es kann ein Wissen vom Teuflischen geben, aber keinen Glauben daran, denn mehr Teuflisches, als da ist, gibt es nicht.

There can be knowledge of the diabolical but not a belief in it, for there cannot be more of the diabolical than does exist.

Recorded on February 21, 1918.

This aphorism clearly describes our relationship to "Evil," since Kafka used the terms "the diabolical" and "Evil" synonymously (see, for example, the precursor to Aphorism 7).

Here it becomes apparent (as it did in Aphorism 48) that Kafka was not using the term "belief" in the merely epistemological sense. He focused not on the ultimately trivial conviction that Evil exists but rather on the question of identification with Evil, which, Kafka claimed, was fundamentally impossible, because it would add new Evil onto the Evil that was already in the world, and this identification would entail a conscious and deliberate absorption of Evil into oneself.

The question arises as to whether Kafka might have landed in a logical pitfall, because if this argument were valid, it would apply to Good as well. Belief in goodness is unquestionably good, so it would add new Good to the Good that already exists in the world—which is impossible according to the line of argument in the aphorism.

Kafka ultimately circumvented this aporia by regarding Good as something more than an opposite of or a counterforce to Evil. Evil is only of transient importance (see Aphorism 54), whereas Good is absolute and eternal, present in full abundance. In this sense there certainly is "more Good than does exist."

Kafka was evidently trying to substantiate his conviction that one can *do* evil things but not *be* utterly and deliberately evil, as this would not be reconcilable with the "indestructible" core of man (see Aphorisms 50 and 70/71). Evil, Aphorism 51 tells us, can "not become man."

For more on Evil, see the commentary on Aphorism 7.

Die Sünde kommt immer offen und ist mit den Sinnen gleich zu fassen. Sie geht auf ihren Wurzeln und muss nicht ausgerissen werden.

Sin always comes openly and can be grasped instantly with the senses. It walks on its roots and needn't be torn out.

Recorded on February 21, 1918. In the octavo notebook, the aphorism reads: "Sin always comes openly and can be grasped instantly with the senses. Transparent, as something self-created. It comes from the outside, and, if asked, names its provenance."

The reformulation on sheet 101 is an example of Kafka's ongoing quest for images that unfolded along with the idea contained within them (as we also see in Aphorism 73). Irrespective of the degree of abstraction in a given idea, Kafka generally favored whichever wording was more vivid and hence more "literary."

In this case, the original version already employed literary devices; Kafka gave sin a speaking role as though it were a human conversant ("if asked, names its provenance"), yet the process remains opaque and leads nowhere. The highly unusual image of roots on which sin "walks," however, compels us to conclude that the far more common metaphor of "tearing out" or "weeding out" of sin misconstrues its true nature.

Two months earlier, Kafka had noted in the octavo notebook: "In Paradise as always: that which causes sin and that which recognizes it for what it is are one and the same." This accords with Kafka's notion that only Evil is aware of moral differences: "Evil knows of Good, but Good does not know of Evil." "Only Evil has self-knowledge." Aphorism 101 draws the conclusion that the person who commits a sin cannot help but notice that he himself is its breeding ground (that it is self-created, as the original version says), even if it appears to come from the outside, for instance in the form of a temptation. Its true roots always remain discernible.

Alle Leiden um uns müssen auch wir leiden. Wir alle haben nicht einen Leib aber ein Wachstum und das führt uns durch alle Schmerzen, ob in dieser oder jener Form. So wie das Kind durch alle Lebensstadien bis zum Greis und zum Tod sich entwickelt (und jedes Stadium im Grunde dem früheren, im Verlangen oder in Furcht, unerreichbar scheint) ebenso entwickeln wir uns (nicht weniger tief mit der Menschheit verbunden als mit uns selbst) durch alle Leiden dieser Welt. Für Gerechtigkeit ist in diesem Zusammenhang kein Platz, aber auch nicht für Furcht vor den Leiden oder für die Auslegung des Leidens als eines Verdienstes.

All the sufferings around us we, too, must suffer. We don't all have one body, but we do have one growth, and that leads us through all pain, in one form or another. Just as a child develops through all the stages of life until old age and death (and each stage seems essentially unattainable to the earlier one, whether in longing or in fear), we develop (no less deeply bound to mankind than to ourselves) through all the sufferings of this world. There is no place for justice in this context, nor is there any place for fear of suffering nor for interpreting suffering as a merit.

Recorded on February 21, 1918. Kafka made several notable revisions to the contents of this aphorism, beginning with the opening sentences, which in the octavo notebook read: "We, too, will have to suffer all the suffering around us. Christ suffered for mankind, but mankind must suffer for Christ. We don't all have one body. . . ." In copying the text onto the sheet, Kafka left out the sentence about Christ, transformed the first sentence from the future to the present tense, and pluralized "suffering."

The phrase "we develop . . . through all the sufferings of this world" was initially followed up in the octavo notebook with the words "until we are all redeemed." Then Kafka amended it to "together with all our fellow men." Neither of these specifications appears in the final version on the sheet.

This aphorism carried forward the idea, formulated on sheet 70/71, that the "indestructible" core of man is more than a merely individual characteristic; there is a single indestructible element that connects all people "indivisibly." As mankind continues to develop, if grievous conflicts and adversities arise in the process, these can neither be avoided nor tackled on an individual level, because they affect absolutely everyone.

In writing the original version of the aphorism, Kafka was presumably inspired by Kierkegaard's *Fear and Trembling* and *Repetition*; according to a note to Max Brod he read both of these works in the second half of February. But even before that, on February 7, a note in the octavo notebook read "Christ, moment," an apparent reference to a key concept in Kierkegaard.

For Kierkegaard, however, "suffering" is a specific, existential, active experience of developing inwardness, while Kafka's aphorism employs the term in a broader sense.

For more on human "development," see also Aphorisms 6 and 54 and the commentary on Aphorism 38. On the subject of human "suffering," see also Aphorisms 97 and 103.

103

Du kannst Dich zurückhalten von den Leiden der Welt, das ist Dir frei-gestellt und entspricht Deiner Natur, aber vielleicht ist gerade dieses Zurück-halten das einzige Leid, das Du vermeiden könntest.

You can withhold yourself from the sufferings of the world; you are free to do so, and it accords with your nature, but perhaps this very act of with-holding is the only suffering you might be able to avoid.

Recorded on February 22, 1918.

This aphorism formulates an idea that can be read as a logical follow-up to the aphorism written just one day earlier: "All the sufferings around us . . ." The wording now becomes "the sufferings of the world." Consequently, Kafka was speaking not of the sufferings that result from random and individual strokes of fate but of the sufferings of mankind, which encompass us all and compel our involvement.

The switch from "we" to "you" signals that Kafka was now intent on drawing ethical conclusions from the insight gained in Aphorism 102. Human nature tends to steer clear of all suffering even from afar, but in losing our connection to suffering as a whole, we might also lose our connection to mankind as such and hence lag behind its development.

This loss of collective experience and connectedness would constitute suffering in the higher sense, which I can avoid by resisting the temptation to retreat, by not isolating myself out of fear of suffering (or fear of the sight of suffering). Aphorism 97 reveals what I ultimately gain by this: I retain the means of participating in the transition into "another world," a world in which experiencing and suffering along with others make for our greatest happiness.

Aphorisms 96, 97, 102, and 103, the four aphorisms that address the subject of suffering, could easily be misunderstood as the expression of an ascetic aversion to the senses or even aversion to happiness if each is considered in isolation (and especially if we bring in the original version of Aphorism 97 as well: "Suffering is the positive element in this world . . ."). But if we contemplate them from the perspective of their mutual relationship, as various angles on one and the same problem, it becomes clear that Kafka had a compassionate form of suffering in mind, the positive, celestial element he sought to preserve.

104

Der Mensch hat freien Willen undzwar dreierlei: Erstens war er frei, als er dieses Leben wollte; jetzt kann er es allerdings nicht mehr rückgängig machen, denn er ist nicht mehr jener, der es damals wollte, es wäre denn insoweit, als er seinen damaligen Willen ausführt, indem er lebt.

Zweitens ist er frei, indem er die Gangart und den Weg dieses Lebens wählen kann.

Drittens ist er frei, indem er als derjenige, der er einmal wieder sein wird, den Willen hat, sich unter jeder Bedingung durch das Leben gehen und auf diese Weise zu sich kommen zu lassen undzwar auf einem zwar wählbaren, aber jedenfalls derartig labyrinthischen Weg, dass er kein Fleckchen dieses Lebens unberührt lässt.

Das ist das Dreierlei des freien Willens, es ist aber auch, da es gleichzeitig ist, ein Einerlei und ist im Grunde so sehr Einerlei, dass es keinen Platz hat für einen Willen weder für einen freien noch unfreien.

Man has free will, of three kinds: First, he was free when he wanted this life; now, though, he cannot go back on it, for he is no longer the one who wanted it back then, unless he could do so to the extent that he carries out his will from back then by living.

Second, he is free in being able to choose the pace and the path of this life.

Third, he is free in having the will, as the one he will someday once again be, to go through life under any circumstance and in this way come to himself, on some path of his own choosing, yet one so very labyrinthine that it leaves not one tiny spot of this life untouched.

Those are the three facets of free will, but it is also—because it is simultaneous—one single facet and is fundamentally so utterly one single facet that it has no place for a will, whether free or unfree.

Recorded on February 22, 1918. The draft in the octavo notebook contains numerous linguistic revisions that were undertaken afterward; these included switching each instance of second-person address ("You were free when you wanted this life . . .") to the third person.

For the initial publication (in the 1931 volume *The Great Wall of China*), this text was incorrectly marked number 89.

This aphorism does not formulate a metaphysical theory but rather describes a train of thought that leads from dissecting a concept ("free will, of three kinds") to the realization that this dissection is pointless. Here we see a reflection of the tentative nature of Kafka's thinking. The following month, when Max Brod lamented in a letter the loss of freedom of the will, Kafka replied, "my eye, which simplifies to the point of complete barrenness, was never able to fix the concept of freedom of the will at a specific point on the horizon as adroitly as you do."

An additional conceptual blurriness arises from the double meaning of "man" as an individual and as a member of the human species. The first of the freedoms named here refers to those who expressed their will to this life on earth in the Fall, and tallies with a statement to Gustav Janouch in which Kafka cites the Fall as evidence that man fundamentally has free will.

The second freedom can be interpreted as an individual one; the third, however, is back to being a collective, because it is not the individual but rather mankind that leaves "not one tiny spot of this life untouched."

The wording "as the one he will someday once again be" is rooted in Kafka's view that man undergoes an "eternal development" (see Aphorism 54) that will lead him out of the earthly bounds. The guarantor of this development is the "indestructible" core of man. Since this indestructible element is both individual and collective (see Aphorism 70/71), the distinction forfeits its metaphysical significance for Kafka—as in this aphorism.

105

Das Verführungsmittel dieser Welt sowie das Zeichen der Bürgschaft dafür, dass diese Welt nur ein Übergang ist, ist das gleiche. Mit Recht denn nur so kann uns diese Welt verführen und es entspricht der Wahrheit. Das Schlimme ist aber, dass wir nach geglückter Verführung die Bürgschaft vergessen und so eigentlich das Gute uns ins Böse, der Blick der Frau in ihr Bett gelockt hat.

The seductiveness of this world and the mark warranting that this world is only a transition are one and the same. Rightly so, for that is the only way this world can seduce us, and it is in keeping with the truth. But the bad thing is that once a seduction has been successful, we forget the warranty, and so Good has lured us into Evil, the woman's gaze into her bed.

Recorded on February 23, 1918. The octavo notebook contains an introductory sentence that Kafka did not include on the sheet: "Woman, or, to express it more pointedly, perhaps, marriage is the representative of life with which you need to come to terms. The bad part is that the means of seduction in this world . . ."

Kafka initially crossed out the idea he had formulated in the last sentence, but then entered it onto the sheet in a more polished form.

The revisions and the image at the end of the aphorism suggest that Kafka was seeking to resume and expand the idea in Aphorism 79: Not only sexual relationships but *all* relationships between a man and a woman—including marriage—are "means of seduction" insofar as they obstruct our view of everything beyond our world of the senses. Still, the only reason they can accomplish this is that they unwittingly hold the transcendent "heavenly" world within them. The promise held out by these relationships ("warranty") is thus a correct one ("in keeping with the truth"). The fault lies with us: When we merely enjoy relationships and settle into them, we forget the promise.

In Aphorism 7, Kafka also spoke about the "means of seduction." Here, too, he chose the bed as an image of defeat. In the ethical abyss between a woman's "gaze" and her "bed" a psychological conflict manifested itself within Kafka, and remained unresolved throughout his life, as evidenced in Aphorism 79, which is thematically related; see the commentary there. Kafka is said to have formulated this contrast even more sharply in a conversation with Gustav Janouch: "Love always inflicts wounds that never really heal, for the appearance of love is always accompanied by filth."

By stating that the world of the senses is only a "transition," Kafka once again asserts that the worlds of the senses and of the spirit are not in static opposition. As Aphorism 54 tells us, the world of the senses is "only a momentary necessity in our eternal development" and consequently doomed to lose out.

106

Die Demut gibt jedem auch dem einsam Verzweifelnden das stärkste Ver-
hältnis zum Mitmenschen undzwar sofort allerdings nur bei völliger und
dauernder Demut. Sie kann das deshalb, weil sie die wahre Gebetsprache ist,
gleichzeitig Anbetung und festeste Verbindung. Das Verhältnis zum Mitmen-
schen ist das Verhältnis des Gebetes, das Verhältnis zu sich das Verhältnis des
Strebens; aus dem Gebet wird die Kraft für das Streben geholt.

Kannst Du denn etwas anderes kennen als Betrug? Wird einmal der Betrug
vernichtet darfst Du ja nicht hinsehn oder Du wirst zur Salzsäule.

Humility gives everyone, even the lonely and despairing, the strongest
bond to their fellow man, instantly, though only if the humility is complete and lasting. It can do so because it is the true language of prayer, at
once worship and the firmest tie. The bond to one's fellow man is the bond
of prayer, the bond to oneself is the bond of striving; it is from prayer that
one draws the strength to strive.

Can you know anything other than deception? If this deception should
ever be destroyed, you won't be able to look or you will turn into a pillar
of salt.

Recorded on February 24, 1918. Kafka copied the second text from a set of later manuscript pages and added to it on the sheet. This second text was written in late August 1920.

Aphorism 70/71 explains why there is invariably a "firmest tie" to one's fellow man: because "the indestructible" is common to us all. The "humility" Kafka endorses simply makes us aware of this tie; it is the form in which even the loneliest among us can become privy to it.

As with the word "belief," Kafka is using the religiously charged term "prayer" to characterize a process or event that can be understood at most *analogously* to religious experience. "Worship" of one's fellow man is not a religious act, just as belief in the "indestructible" is not religious belief (see the commentaries on aphorisms 50 and 109).

Aphorism 106 depicts an *inner* disposition to one's fellow man. With respect to concrete social conduct, however, Kafka tried to convince himself that it could not be right to acquiesce to others and strain to be understandable ("visible") at any cost merely in order to ensure that communication doesn't break off. He illustrated this stance two years later with the image of the solitary Robinson Crusoe. Here again, he employed the word "humility," but this time in a negative sense: "If Robinson had never left the . . . most visible point of the island, out of defiance or humility or fear or ignorance or longing, he would soon have perished, but since he began to explore his whole island, without regard for the ships and their weak telescopes, and started to take pleasure in doing so, he kept himself alive."

As for the second text: The analysis of a moral problem in Aphorism 55 provides a concrete example of how, from a human perspective, everything becomes a deception. The truth that lies beyond deception is in the "world of the spirit" and hence remains fundamentally unattainable, even by means of art (see Aphorisms 57 and 63). The augmented text, on sheet 99, even refers to a "great primal deception."

107

Alle sind zu A. sehr freundlich, so etwa wie man ein ausgezeichnetes Billard selbst vor guten Spielern sorgfältig zu bewahren sucht, solange bis der grosse Spieler kommt, das Brett genau untersucht, keinen vorzeitigen Fehler duldet, dann aber, wenn er selbst zu spielen anfängt, sich auf die rücksichtsloseste Weise auswütet.

Everyone is very friendly to A., rather in the way one takes care to shield an excellent billiard table from even good players until the great player comes, thoroughly examines the table, tolerates no prior flaws, but then, when he himself begins to play, runs riot in the most reckless manner.

Recorded on February 26, 1918.

Even as a schoolboy, Kafka was convinced that he was able to muddle through school and get promoted to each subsequent grade only because of the kindness and indulgence shown by other people, and that the hoax would be exposed instantly if put to any serious test. He continued to cling to this belief while working as an official at the Workers' Accident Insurance Institute. There, too, Kafka feared that his solid, almost friendly relationship with his supervisors was possible only because they turned a blind eye to the inadequacy of his achievements. The inevitable approach of a "true" test remained one of Kafka's most persistent and agonizing visions for decades. (He employed a creative defensive strategy of making himself small; see Aphorism 90).

Aphorism 107 sublimates this notion into "play," but at the same time lends it a positively mythical ramification. It suggests that the friendliness of others serves the sole purpose of preparing the victim, "A.," for the appearance of the "great player," who will show no consideration and will subject the billiard table to a sadistic test. (Kafka's use of the definite article ["*the* great player"] underscores the intended mythicizing effect.)

This aphorism is one of the many examples of how Kafka transports an emphatically and psychologically comprehensible experience into a quasi-mythical notion, which then takes on literary form. The fate of Josef K., the accused man in *The Trial*, is one instance that could be read as a "true test," one that renders meaningless all the exams he has passed in his life.

In billiards, *Brett* is a less common synonym for *Tisch* (table). For more on the abbreviation "A.," see the commentary on Aphorism 10.

108

"Dann aber kehrte er zu seiner Arbeit zurück, so wie wenn nichts geschehen wäre." Das ist eine Bemerkung, die uns aus einer unklaren Fülle alter Erzählungen geläufig ist, trotzdem sie vielleicht in keiner vorkommt.

"But then he returned to his work as though nothing had happened." We are familiar with this kind of remark from any number of old tales, even though it may not be found in any of them.

Recorded on February 26, 1918.

Kafka cites an example to demonstrate that things (as well as people) have an intrinsic nature, a kind of spiritual essence. The quoted sentence is "familiar" to us not because we recognize its wording from something we have read but rather because it is well suited to capture the essence of the world of "old tales"—their atmosphere, their characteristic simplicity, et cetera—which is why the sentence sounds not only right but apparently recognizable; a mental reinforcement takes place, with no need for an exact factual accord.

109

"Dass es uns an Glauben fehle, kann man nicht sagen. Allein die einfache Tatsache unseres Lebens ist in ihrem Glaubenswert gar nicht auszuschöpfen." "Hier wäre ein Glaubenswert? Man kann doch nicht nicht-leben." "Eben in diesem 'kann doch nicht' steckt die wahnsinnige Kraft des Glaubens; in dieser Verneinung bekommt sie Gestalt."

Es ist nicht notwendig, dass Du aus dem Haus gehst. Bleib bei Deinem Tisch und horche. Horche nicht einmal, warte nur. Warte nicht einmal, sei völlig still und allein. Anbieten wird sich Dir die Welt zur Entlarvung, sie kann nicht anders, verzückt wird sie sich vor Dir winden.

"It cannot be said that we lack in belief. The very fact that we live at all is an inexhaustible wellspring of belief."

"This would indicate a wellspring of belief? Surely one cannot *not* live."

"The incredible power of belief lies squarely in that 'surely one cannot'; it takes on its form in this negation."

It is not necessary for you to leave the house. Stay at your table and listen. Don't even listen; just wait. Don't even wait; be utterly still and alone. The world will offer itself to you to be unmasked; it cannot do otherwise; it will writhe before you in ecstasy.

The first text was recorded on February 26, 1918. Kafka copied the second text from a set of later manuscript pages and added to it on the sheet. This second text was written in late August 1920.

The Zürau octavo notebooks contain several dialogue fragments, but Aphorism 109 is the only one formulated as a dialogue. The process by which Kafka arrived at this decision is easy to retrace with the aid of the octavo notebooks, where we find two earlier wordings that are not in the form of a dialogue.

Kafka blanketed the first version with so many revisions that the text became virtually unreadable, and he found it necessary to copy and continue to revise it: "Every person is asked two questions regarding belief here, first as to the believability of this life, second as to the believability of his goal. Both questions are answered by every person, by the very fact of his life, with such a firm and quick 'yes' that it could become uncertain whether the questions had even been understood correctly. In any case, one has to begin to work one's way through to this, one's own basic Yes. . . ."

The copy remained incomplete, however; this is evidently the exact place that Kafka hit upon the idea of introducing two nameless speakers to allow for a far more trenchant portrayal of the two stages of reflection: the hasty, impetuous Yes to life (the "basic Yes") and the deliberate "working one's way through" to the underlying impulse.

Aphorism 109 confirms once more that "belief" can remain unconscious or at least rest on bases that remain unconscious (analogously to Aphorism 50). "Belief" in the sense of Kafka's definition is therefore not synonymous with religious belief but with something more along the lines of "devotion" or "complete identification." Kafka held in high regard the ability to achieve this kind of belief, independently of its contents. He had noted in his diary in 1914: "Karlsbad [i.e., the spa facility there] is a greater swindle than Lourdes, and Lourdes has the advantage that people are inspired to go there by their innermost belief." (On the use of religious terms, see also Aphorism 106.)

In the second text, Kafka initially wrote: "Don't even listen, wait until it pressures you." In copying this text onto the sheet, he reworded it to read, "Don't even listen, just wait." The surprise twist—the world's offering of itself—is thus shifted into the final sentence, evidently to heighten its dramatic impact.

The key point in this text is Kafka's endorsement of contemplation, a meditative stance, as opposed to reflection, although "unmasking" is actually a reflective, intellectual activity. In order to adopt an observational position toward the world of the senses, however, it is first essential to disentangle ourselves from this world, including the tools we normally activate in pursuit of knowledge, such as language; see Aphorism 57.

This text can be read as self-admonition but also as a guide for readers seeking to foster their own awareness, so it may be no coincidence that Kafka added to it on the very last of his sheets, as if intending it to serve as the closing words of an intended publication of the aphorisms.

Abbreviations

8°Ox7   *Oxforder Oktavheft 7* [Oxford octavo notebook 7]. *Historisch-Kritische Ausgabe sämtlicher Handschriften, Drucke und Typoskripte,* ed. Roland Reuß and Peter Staengle. Frankfurt am Main: Stroemfeld/Roter Stern, 2011.

8°Ox8   *Oxforder Oktavheft 8* [Oxford octavo notebook 8]. *Historisch-Kritische Ausgabe sämtlicher Handschriften, Drucke und Typoskripte,* ed. Roland Reuß and Peter Staengle. Frankfurt am Main: Stroemfeld/Roter Stern, 2011.

B1   *Briefe 1900–1912* [Letters, 1900–1912], ed. Hans-Gerd Koch. Frankfurt am Main: S. Fischer, 1999.

B2   *Briefe 1913–1914* [Letters, 1913–1914], ed. Hans-Gerd Koch. Frankfurt am Main: S. Fischer, 2001.

B3   *Briefe 1914–1917* [Letters, 1914–1917], ed. Hans-Gerd Koch. Frankfurt am Main: S. Fischer, 2005.

B4   *Briefe 1918–1920* [Letters, 1918–1920], ed. Hans-Gerd Koch. Frankfurt am Main: S. Fischer, 2013.

D   *Drucke zu Lebzeiten* [Writings published during his lifetime], ed. Wolf Kittler, Hans-Gerd Koch, and Gerhard Neumann. Frankfurt am Main: S. Fischer, 1994.

NSF1   *Nachgelassene Schriften und Fragmente I* [Unpublished writings and fragments 1], ed. Malcolm Pasley. Frankfurt am Main: S. Fischer, 1993.

NSF2   *Nachgelassene Schriften und Fragmente II* [Unpublished writings and fragments 2], ed. Jost Schillemeit. Frankfurt am Main: S. Fischer, 1992.

P   *Der Proceß* [The trial], ed. Malcolm Pasley. Frankfurt am Main: S. Fischer, 1990.

S   *Das Schloß* [The castle], ed. Malcolm Pasley. Frankfurt am Main: S. Fischer, 1982.

T   *Tagebücher* [Diaries], ed. Hans-Gerd Koch, Michael Müller, and Malcolm Pasley. Frankfurt am Main: S. Fischer, 1990.

Notes

The numbers in the left column refer to the aphorisms. The first line of each reference is in bold to show that it cites the source of the aphorism itself; the information that follows, not in bold, refers to the commentary for each aphorism on the recto side.

1   **NSF2 30, 113 / 8°Ox7 8**
    Das Jüdische Echo (Munich), no. 38, September 21, 1917, 423. *NSF2* 48, 55, 105, 112 / *8°Ox7* 72, 95; *8°Ox8* 88–91, 111. Letter to Robert Klopstock, July 24, 1922 (Franz Kafka, *Briefe 1902–1924*, ed. Max Brod [Frankfurt am Main: S. Fischer, 1975], 398). The prose piece "A Commentary" was written between mid-November and mid-December 1922.

2   **NSF2 32, 113 / 8°Ox7 16**
    Letter from Felix Weltsch to Kafka, 3rd week of October, 1917 (*B3* 762ff.). Letter to Felix Weltsch, October 19–21, 1917 (*B3* 353f.). *Die literarische Welt* (Berlin), June 4, 1926 (issue devoted to Kafka on the occasion of the second anniversary of his death).

3   **NSF2 32f., 113 / 8°Ox7 19**
    Postcard to Felice Bauer, September 10, 1916 (*B3* 219). *NSF2* 65, 72, 73, 77, 78 / *8°Ox7* 124, 140, 140–143, 156, 159f.

4   **NSF2 33f., 114 / 8°Ox7 23**
    NSF1 309.

5   **NSF2 34, 114 / 8°Ox7 23**
    Diary, January 19, 1922 (*T* 881).

6   **NSF2 34, 114 / 8°Ox7 23f.**
    Letter to Max Brod, November 6, 1917 (*B3* 360).

7   **NSF2 34f., 114 / 8°Ox7 24–26**
    NSF2 48f., 57, 66, 73 / *8°Ox7* 75, 100, 124, 144.

8/9 **NSF2 37, 115 / 8°Ox7 36**

10 **NSF2 39, 115 / 8°Ox7 43f.**
    NSF2 38, 48 / *8°Ox7* 39f., 75. Diary, July 9, 1912 (*T* 426). *NSF2* 104 / *8°Ox8* 87.

11/12 **NSF2 115f., NSF2 Apparatband 205 / 8°Ox7 44**
    Letter to Milena Jesenská, August 13, 1920 (*B4* 308f.).

13 **NSF2 43, 116 / 8°Ox7 63**
    Diary, July 22, 1916 (*T* 800f.). *NSF2* 76 / *8°Ox7* 155. Diary, January 13, 1920; February 19, 1920; and October 21, 1921 (*T* 849, 859, 869).

14 **NSF2 44, 116 / 8°Ox7 63f.**
    NSF2 44 / *8°Ox7* 64. Diary, before July 13, 1916 (*T* 795). The Swiss girl in Riva mentioned here lived in Italy. Riva still belonged to Austria-Hungary.

15 **NSF2 44, 117 / 8°Ox7 64**

16 **NSF2 44, 117 / 8°Ox7 64**

17 **NSF2 45, 117 / 8°Ox7 67**
    NSF2 49 / *8°Ox7* 76. *NSF2* 57 / *8°Ox7* 100. Letter to Max Brod, ca. March 5, 1918 (*B4* 31). Letter to Oskar Baum, late March/early April 1918 (*B4* 38). Diary, January 24, 1922 (*T* 889).

18   *NSF2* 45, 117 / *8°Ox7* 67
Micha Josef bin Gorion. *Die Sagen der Juden*, vol. 2: *Die Erzväter*. Frankfurt
am Main: Rütten & Loening, 1914, pp. 61ff. Postcard to Max Brod, August 29,
1917 (*B3* 310). *NSF2* 484.

19   *NSF2* 45, 117 / *8°Ox7* 67f.
Letter to Max Brod, September 14, 1917 (*B3* 319).

20   *NSF2* 46, 117 / *8°Ox7* 68
Diary, June 2, 1916 (*T* 788). See Nathan Söderblom, *Das Werden des Gottes-
glaubens: Untersuchungen über die Anfänge der Religion* (Leipzig: J. C. Hinrichs:
1916), 117.

21   *NSF2* 46, 118 / *8°Ox7* 68
Letter to Max Brod, May 27, 1910 (*B1* 121f.). *NSF2* 31 / *8°Ox7* 11.

22   *NSF2* 46, 118 / *8°Ox7* 68
Letter to Max Brod, September 14, 1917 (*B3* 319). Letter to Milena Jesenská,
October 7, 1920 (*B4* 355). *NSF2* 71 / *8°Ox7* 136. Diary, January 21, 1922 (*T* 884).

23   *NSF2* 46, 118 / *8°Ox7* 71
Letter to Max Brod, October 7 or 8, 1917; see the letter from Brod to Kafka,
October 4, 1917 (*B3* 342, 753f.). *NSF2* 153f.

24   *NSF2* 46, 118 / *8°Ox7* 71
Letter to Felice Bauer, April 20, 1915 (*B3* 129). Diary, Fall 1910 (*T* 118).
NSF2 98, *8°Ox8* 64. Letter to Max Brod, July 5, 1922 (*Max Brod/Franz Kafka:
Eine Freundschaft—Briefwechsel*, ed. Malcolm Pasley [Frankfurt am Main:
S. Fischer, 1989], 377, 378f.).

25   *NSF2* 47, 118 / *8°Ox7* 71
Letter to Felice Bauer, March 16–17, 1913 (*B2* 137). Diary, March 15, 1922
(*T* 912).

26   *NSF2* 47, 118, 322 / *8°Ox7* 71 / *8°Ox8* 141.
Letter to Max Brod, November 6, 1917 (*B3* 360). Diary, September 28, 1915
(*T* 755).

27   *NSF2* 47, 119 / *8°Ox7* 71

28   *NSF2* 48, 119 / *8°Ox7* 75

29   *NSF2* 48, 119, 344 / *8°Ox7* 75 / *8°Ox8* 144.
Diary, February 7, 1915 (*T* 725). Letter to Milena Jesenská, November 3, 1920
(*B4* 366). Diary, October 16, 1916 (*T* 805).

30   *NSF2* 49, 119 / *8°Ox7* 76
NSF2 48 / *8°Ox7* 75. *NSF2* 73 / *8°Ox7* 144.

31   *NSF2* 50f., 119f. / *8°Ox7* 80
Diary, October 16, 1916 (*T* 805). Letter to Max Brod, December 10, 1917
(*B3* 379).

32   *NSF2* 51, 120 / *8°Ox7* 80–83
Letter to Felice Bauer, November 26, 1912 (*B1* 273). The hearing had taken
place at the district court in Kratzau, on the outskirts of Reichenberg. Kafka
was reluctant primarily because he had to interrupt his writing of "The Metamorphosis" for this business trip. *S* 17.

33   *NSF2* 51, 120 / *8°Ox7* 83
NSF2 52f. / *8°Ox7* 88.

34   *NSF2* 51, 120 / *8°Ox7* 83
Letter to Max Brod, September 14, 1917 (*B3* 320). "The New Attorney" was
published as the opening text in the volume *A Country Doctor* (1920) but first

saw print even earlier, in mid-September 1917, as a preprint in the journal *Marsyas* (Berlin), just as Kafka was moving to Zürau. Letter to Käthe Nettel, November 24, 1919 (*B4* 90).

35   *NSF2* 52, 120 / *8°Ox7* 84–87
   Letter to Felix Weltsch, between October 19 and 21, 1917 (*B3* 353).

36   *NSF2* 52, 120f. / *8°Ox7* 87
   Diary, September 28, 1915 (*T* 755). Letter to Oskar Baum, mid-June 1920 (*B4* 182). Diary, October 15, 1921 (*T* 863).

37   *NSF2* 52, 121 / *8°Ox7* 87f.
   NSF2 55 / *8°Ox7* 95

38   *NSF2* 53, 121 / *8°Ox7* 88
   NSF1 309. Letter to Max Brod, September 14, 1917 (*B3* 320). *NSF2* 78 / *8°Ox7* 159.

39   *NSF2* 53, 121, 322 / *8°Ox7* 88 / *8°Ox8* 141.
   Gustav Janouch, *Gespräche mit Kafka: Aufzeichnungen und Erinnerungen,* expanded ed. (Frankfurt am Main: S. Fischer, 1968), 60. *NSF2* 31 / *8°Ox7* 12–15.

39a *NSF2* 53, 121 / *8°Ox7* 91
   Letter to Felice Bauer, July 16, 1916 (*B3* 176). Letter to Milena Jesenská, ca. May 12, 1920 (*B4* 135).

40   *NSF2* 54, 122 / *8°Ox7* 91
   NSF2 62 / *8°Ox7* 116.—The fragment "The Knock at the Manor Gate," which was originally untitled, begins with the words "It was summer, a hot day" (*NSF1* 361–363). Diary, January 29, 1922 (*T* 896).

41   *NSF2* 54, 122 / *8°Ox7* 92
   Diary, August 21, 1913 (*T* 568–570). Letter to Felice Bauer, December 29, 1913, to January 2, 1914 (*B2* 310).

42   *NSF2* 54, 122 / *8°Ox7* 92
   Letter to Max Brod, August 28, 1904 (*B1* 40). Diary, November 5, 1911 (*T* 226). This comment refers to a literary text about a car accident Kafka witnessed in Paris; Max Brod read this "story" aloud in Kafka's presence. *D* 53. *S* 15.

43   *NSF2* 55, 122 / *8°Ox7* 95f.
   Letter to Minze Eisner, mid-January 1920 (*B4* 96). Diary, January 16, 1922 (*T* 878). *NSF1* 311, 309. *NSF2* 26f. Postcard to Robert Klopstock, July 13, 1923 (Kafka, *Briefe*, 435).

44   *NSF2* 56, 122 / *8°Ox7* 96
45   *NSF2* 56, 123 / *8°Ox7* 96
   Letters to Max Brod, September 18, 1917; and March 26–27, 1918 (*B3* 324, *B4* 33).

46   *NSF2* 56, 123 / *8°Ox7* 96
   Diary, May 4, 1915; November 24, 1911 (*T* 743, 266). Letter to Felice Bauer, December 27–28, 1912 (*B1* 366).

47   *NSF2* 56, 123 / *8°Ox7* 96–99
   D 252. *P* 101ff. *S* 408ff.

48   *NSF2* 57, 123 / *8°Ox7* 99
   NSF2 455.

49   *NSF2* 57, 123 / *8°Ox7* 99f.
   D 356, 355.

50   *NSF2* 58, 124 / *8°Ox7* 100
51   *NSF2* 58, 124 / *8°Ox7* 103

NSF2 65 / 8°Ox7 124. NSF2 73 / 8°Ox7 140–143. NSF2 75 / 8°Ox7 152. NSF2 42 / 8°Ox7 55f.

52 **NSF2 58, 124 / 8°Ox7 103**
Diary, January 16, 1922 (*T* 878).

53 **NSF2 58, 124 / 8°Ox7 103**
Letter to Max Brod, November 14, 1917 (*B3* 362f.).

54 **NSF2 59, 124, 322 / 8°Ox7 103 / 8°Ox8 143.**

55 **NSF2 59, 125 / 8°Ox7 103f.**

56 **NSF2 59, 125 / 8°Ox7 107**

57 **NSF2 59, 126 / 8°Ox7 107**
NSF2 50 / 8°Ox7 80.

58 **NSF2 60, 126 / 8°Ox7 107**
Diary, August 30, 1913 (*T* 581). Letter to Milena Jesenská, November 26, 1920 (*B4* 373).

59 **NSF2 60, 126 / 8°Ox7 111**

60 **NSF2 61, 126 / 8°Ox7 112**

61 **NSF2 61, 126f. / 8°Ox7 112**
NSF2 61 / 8°Ox7 111f.

62 **NSF2 61, 127 / 8°Ox7 115**
Max Brod, *Über Franz Kafka* (Frankfurt am Main: S. Fischer, 1974), 71.

63 **NSF2 62, 127 / 8°Ox7 115**
NSF2 57f. / 8°Ox7 148. Letter to Max Brod, October 22–24, 1923 (Pasley, *Max Brod/Franz Kafka*, 435).

64 **NSF2 62, 127 / 8°Ox7 115f.**
NSF2 62 / 8°Ox7 116.

66 **NSF2 63, 127f. / 8°Ox7 119f.**

67 **NSF2 64, 128 / 8°Ox7 123**
Letter to Felice Bauer, June 8–16, 1913 (*B2* 209).

68 **NSF2 65, 128 / 8°Ox7 123**
Diary, February 1, 1922 (*T* 899).

69 **NSF2 65, 128 / 8°Ox7 123**
NSF2 55 / 8°Ox7 95. Letter to Max Brod, August 6, 1920 (*B4* 285). Letter to Felice Bauer, March 9, 1913 (*B2* 127).

70/71 **NSF2 66, 128 / 8°Ox7 124**
NSF2 55 / 8°Ox7 95.

72 **NSF2 66, 129 / 8°Ox7 127**

73 **NSF2 67, 129 / 8°Ox7 127**

74 **NSF2 67, 129 / 8°Ox7 128**
NSF2 72 / 8°Ox7 139.

75 **NSF2 67, 129 / 8°Ox7 128**

76 **NSF2 68, 129, 279 / 8°Ox7 128 / 8°Ox8 138.**
Brod, *Über Franz Kafka*, 147. According to Brod's unpublished diaries, Kafka made this comment on December 26, 1917.

77 **NSF2 68, 130 / 8°Ox7 128**
Diary, December 9, 1913 (*T* 608). NSF2 42 / 8°Ox7 55f. Diary, November 7, 1921; January 16, 1922; March 9, 1922 (*T* 874, 877, 910).

78 **NSF2 68, 130 / 8°Ox7 128**
NSF2 105 / 8°Ox8 88–91.

79   *NSF2* **68, 130** / *8°Ox7* **131**
      Letter to Max Brod, January 20, 1918 (*B4* 23). Letter to Milena Jesenská,
      August 9, 1920 (*B4* 297f.).
80   *NSF2* **69, 130** / *8°Ox7* **131**
      NSF2 48 / *8°Ox7* 75. *NSF2* 73 / *8°Ox7* 144. Letter to Max Brod, July 20, 1922
      (Pasley, *Max Brod/Franz Kafka,* 390).
81   *NSF2* **69, 130f.** / *8°Ox7* **132**
      Postcard to Willy Haas, July 19, 1912 (*B1* 162).
82   *NSF2* **71, 131** / *8°Ox7* **136-139**
      Genesis 3:22-23 (NIV).
83   *NSF2* **72, 131** / *8°Ox7* **139**
      NSF2 83f. / *8°Ox8* 16-19.
84   *NSF2* **72, 131** / *8°Ox7* **139f.**
      NSF2 72f. / *8°Ox7* 139f.
85   *NSF2* **74, 132** / *8°Ox7* **144**
86   *NSF2* **74f., 132f.** / *8°Ox7* **147-152**
87   *NSF2* **76, 133** / *8°Ox7* **148**
88   *NSF2* **76, 133** / *8°Ox7* **155**
      Letter to Max Brod, September 28, 1917 (*B3* 331). Diary, September 28, 1917
      (*T* 839).
90   *NSF2* **78, 133** / *8°Ox7* **156-159**
      Letter to Felice Bauer, May 15, 1913 (*B2* 189); Letter to Milena Jesenská, July 18,
      1920 (*B4* 233).
91   *NSF2* **78, 133** / *8°Ox7* **159**
92   *NSF2* **79, 134** / *8°Ox8* **4**
93   *NSF2* **81, 134** / *8°Ox8* **8**
      Briefe von und an J.M.R. Lenz, ed. Karl Freye and Wolfgang Stammler, 2 vols.,
      (Leipzig: Kurt Wolff, [1918], 1969). *NSF2* 100 / *8°Ox8* 72. *NSF2* 35 / *8°Ox7* 16
      (note dated October 19, 1917). Letter to Max Brod, November 14, 1917
      (*B4* 364f.).
94   *NSF2* **81, 134** / *8°Ox8* **8**
      NSF2 99 / *8°Ox8* 68-71. Diary, January 3, 1912 (*T* 341).
95   *NSF2* **81, 134f.** / *8°Ox8* **8-11**
      Max Brod's diary entry is dated July 3, 1918 (Kafka's 35th birthday), and is
      quoted in Brod, *Über Franz Kafka,* 149.
96   *NSF2* **81, 135** / *8°Ox8* **11**
97   *NSF2* **83, 135** / *8°Ox8* **15**
      Letter to Max Brod, March 26 or 27, 1918 (*B4* 34).
98   *NSF2* **84, 135** / *8°Ox8* **19**
99   *NSF2* **89, 135f., 253** / *8°Ox8* **32-35, 134-137.**
      NSF2 88f. / *8°Ox8* 32. *NSF2* 62 / *8°Ox7* 116.
100   *NSF2* **93, 136** / *8°Ox8* **47f.**
101   *NSF2* **93, 136** / *8°Ox8* **48**
      NSF2 66 / *8°Ox7* 124. *NSF2* 48 / *8°Ox7* 75.
102   *NSF2* **93f., 137** / *8°Ox8* **48-51**
      Letter to Max Brod, ca. March 5, 1918 (*B4* 30). *NSF2* 87 / *8°Ox8* 28.
103   *NSF2* **94, 137** / *8°Ox8* **52**
      NSF2 83 / *8°Ox8* 12.

104 *NSF2* 94f., 137f. / *8°Ox8* 55f.
   Letter to Max Brod, March 26 or 27, 1918 (*T* 33). Janouch, *Gespräche mit Kafka*, 125.

105 *NSF2* 95f., 137f. / *8°Ox8* 56–59
   Janouch, *Gespräche mit Kafka*, 100.

106 *NSF2* 96, 138f., 253 / *8°Ox8* 59f., 137
   Diary, February 18, 1920 (*T* 859).

107 *NSF2* 101, 139 / *8°Ox8* 76

108 *NSF2* 101, 139 / *8°Ox8* 76–79

109 *NSF2* 102f., 139f., 254 / *8°Ox8* 80–83, 137
   NSF2 102 / *8°Ox8* 80. Diary, February 2, 1914 (*T* 632).

Bibliography

Alt, Peter-André. *Franz Kafka: Der ewige Sohn*. Munich: C. H. Beck, 2005, 460–469.

Binder, Hartmut, ed. *Kafka-Handbuch in Zwei Bänden*. Vol. 2: *Das Werk und seine Wirkung*. Stuttgart: Kröner, 1979, 474–497.

Cavarocchi Arbib, Maria. "Jüdische Motive in Kafkas Aphorismen." In Karl Erich Grözinger, Stéphane Mosès, and Hans Dieter Zimmermann, eds. *Kafka und das Judentum*. Frankfurt am Main: Athenäum, 1987, 122–146.

Citati, Pietro. *Kafka: Verwandlungen eines Dichters*. Munich: Piper, 1990, 182–206.

Dietzfelbinger, Konrad. *Kafkas Geheimnis: Eine Interpretation von Franz Kafkas Betrachtungen über Sünde, Leid, Hoffnung und den wahren Weg*. Freiburg im Breisgau: Aurum, 1987.

Engel, Manfred, and Bernd Auerochs, eds. *Kafka-Handbuch: Leben—Werk—Wirkung*. Stuttgart: J. B. Metzler, 2010, 281–292.

Gray, Richard. *Constructive Deconstruction: Kafka's Aphorisms: Literary Tradition and Literary Transformation*. Tübingen: M. Niemeyer, 1987.

———. "The Literary Sources of Kafka's Aphoristic Impulse." *Literary Review* 26 (1983), 537–550.

———. "Suggestive Metaphor: Kafka's Aphorisms and the Crisis of Communication." *Deutsche Vierteljahresschrift für Literaturwissenschaft und Geistesgeschichte* 58 (1984), 454–469.

Hoffmann, Werner. *Kafkas Aphorismen*. Bern: Francke, 1975.

Kaszynski, Stefan H. "Kafkas Kunst des Aphorismus." In Stefan H. Kaszynski, *Österreich und Mitteleuropa: Kritische Seitenblicke auf die neuere österreichische Literatur*. Poznan: Uniwersytet im. Adama Mickiewicza w Poznaniu, 1975, 73–105.

———. "Die Realität der Symbole im Aphorismenwerk von Franz Kafka." In Stefan H. Kaszynski, *Kleine Geschichte des österreichischen Aphorismus*. Tübingen: A. Francke, 1999, 93–102.

Krystofiak, Maria. "Kafkas Aphorismen im Dialog mit Kierkegaard." In Sigurd Paul Scheichl, ed. *Feuilleton—Essay—Aphorismus: Nichtfiktionale Prosa in Österreich*. Innsbruck: Innsbruck University Press, 2008, 161–171.

Lawson, Richard H. "Kafka and Canetti: The Art of Writing, as Mediated by Aphorism." In Frank Philipp, ed. *The Legacy of Kafka in Contemporary Austrian Literature*. Riverside: Ariadne Press, 1997, 31–42.

Milfull, Helen. "The Theological Position of Franz Kafka's Aphorisms." *Seminar* 18 (1982), 169–183.

North, Paul. *The Yield: Kafka's Atheological Reformation*. Palo Alto: Stanford University Press, 2015.

Robertson, Ritchie. *Kafka: Judaism, Politics, Literature*. Oxford: Clarendon Press, 1985, 185–217.

———. "Kafka as Anti-Christian: *Das Urteil, Die Verwandlung*, and the Aphorisms." In James Rolleston, ed. *A Companion to the Works of Franz Kafka*. New York: Camden House, 2002, 101–122.

———. "Kafka's Zürau Aphorisms." In *Oxford German Studies* 14 (1983), 73–91.

Sandbank, Shimon. "Surprise Technique in Kafka's Aphorisms." *Orbis litterarum*, 25 (1970), 261–274.

Sedelnik, Wladimir. "Franz Kafkas Aphorismen und das (post)moderne Denken." In Wolfgang Kraus and Norbert Winkler, eds. *Das Phänomen Franz Kafka: Vorträge des Symposions der Österreichischen Franz Kafka-Gesellschaft in Klosterneuburg 1995.* Prague: Vitalis, 1997, 59–73.

Stach, Reiner. *Kafka: The Years of Insight.* Shelley Frisch, trans. Princeton: Princeton University Press, 2013, 222–243.

Topa, Maria Helena. "Notas para estudio da aforística de Franz Kafka: Perspectivismo e ficcionalidade." *Runa* 13/14 (1990), 81–87.

Weltsch, Felix. "Kafkas Aphorismen." *Deutsche Hefte* 1 (1954/55), 307–312.